Winnie
the
horse gentler
I0816058

Winnie the horse gentler Devotional

30 New Stories for Horse-Loving Readers

Dandi Daley Mackall

Tyndale House Publishers
Carol Stream, Illinois

Visit Tyndale online at tyndale.com.

Visit Tyndale's website for kids at tyndale.com/kids.

Visit the author online at dandibooks.com.

Winnie the Horse Gentler Devotional: 30 New Stories for Horse-Loving Readers

Designed by Jacqueline L. Nuñez

Edited by Deborah King

For manufacturing information regarding this product, please call 1-855-277-9400.

For information about special discounts for bulk purchases, please contact Tyndale House Publishers at csresponse@tyndale.com, or call 1-855-277-9400.

ISBN 978-1-4964-9054-4

Printed in India

31 30 29 28 27 26 25
7 6 5 4 3 2 1

To my husband, Joe, God's gracious gift to me:
Thanks, my Love!

You care for people and animals alike, O Lord.
Psalm 36:6

Contents

Author's Note

It's such an honor to write a book as if I'm Winnie the Horse Gentler working life out with God . . . and horses—the way I guess I've done my whole life. Much like Winnie, I grew up with horses as my best friends. I admit there are many pieces of me and my horses in the Winnie books.

The first book about Winnie the Horse Gentler, *Wild Thing*, released in 2002, followed by seven other Winnie novels. I'm thankful for the great letters and emails Winnie and I have received since then.

Over the years, new generations of readers have befriended Winnie. So I let Winnie make appearances in Starlight Animal Rescue, and I added a new series, Winnie: The Early Years.

You don't need to know anything about Winnie to read this book, but here's a peek into her world.

Who's Who in Winnie's World

Winnie—Winifred Willis (Winnie) is in eighth grade. She grew up on a ranch in Wyoming, where her mom taught her how to gentle horses rather than break them. After her mom died, Winnie's dad moved his two daughters all over the US, finally landing in Ashland, Ohio. People bring Winnie their problem horses, and she gentles them with kindness. Winnie is great with horses—not so much with humans, especially certain classmates. But from day to day, she discovers she can apply her horse knowledge to people. School cliques aren't that different from Mustang herds, after all.

Nickers—Winnie's white Arabian had earned the name Wild Thing when the Spidells gave up on her and wanted her out of Spidell's Stable-Mart. They had tried to break her with *no* gentleness, just frustrating punishment. Winnie ended up with Wild Thing and helped her become Nickers instead, which is a soft sound from a horse, the sweetest music on earth.

Lizzy—Elizabeth Priscilla Willis (Lizzy) is a year younger than her sister, Winnie. She's taller than Winnie, maybe more mature, and has a solid and fun relationship with God. She's not crazy about horses but loves lizards.

Jack Willis—Winnie's dad used to be the boss in a Wyoming insurance company. When his wife died, he quit because he couldn't stay where sad memories lurked. Moving with his daughters from state to state, he worked at odd jobs wherever he could. Knowing Winnie needed horses, he rented the last farmhouse at the edge of Ashland, Ohio, which came with an old barn and an overgrown pasture. Now he pursues his passion of inventing things, like the Backwards Bike.

Catman—Calvin Coolidge (Catman) is a throwback to hippies, with expressions like "Far out!" "Groovy," and "Cool, man." He could be a cat whisperer because cats follow him everywhere. Catman's parents are "far out," entering contests for a living and decorating year-round with lawn ornaments. Catman is probably Winnie's best friend.

Barker—Eddy Barker (Barker) loves dogs and knows all about them, training dogs for his family and friends, as well as training police dogs and service dogs. The Barkers are a wonderful African American family, including Granny B. and Barker's great granny, "Ma Barker," who seems out of it until she reveals her wisdom. Each of Barker's five brothers has his own dog, trained by Eddy.

M—Nobody knows what the M stands for, with the possible exception of Catman, M's best buddy. M doesn't say much, but he communicates, sometimes by eating sandwiches in the shape of his message. He always wears black . . . until someone comes up with a darker color. Catman and M help Winnie whenever she needs them.

Hawk—Victoria Hawkins (Hawk) is a Native American classmate who loves birds, owns an Appaloosa named Towaco, and has to split her time between parents, now that they're divorced. Formerly best friend to Summer Spidell, Hawk began as Winnie's un-friend but has become her best on-and-off female friend.

Pat—Pat Haven owns Pat's Pets, the town pet store. She oversees the online Pet Helpline run by Winnie, Catman, Barker, and sometimes Hawk. People (kids too) email with animal problems. Winnie answers horse questions, Catman gets cat problems, Barker takes dog questions, and they call in Hawk for an occasional bird problem.

Summer and the Spidells—Summer Spidell comes from money. She only rides horses from her dad's stable, Stable-Mart, so she can win trophies in horse shows. A classmate of Winnie's, Summer is often her enemy, as is Summer's older brother, Robert.

Parts of Each Devotion

Each devotional begins with a verse that expresses the main idea of the story. As Winnie comes to understand the verse (or fails to), she discovers how the Treasure Verse applies to her on a deeper, more personal level.

Here are some other features you'll see regularly in each devotional:

Winnie's Story—Winnie the Horse Gentler understands horses better than she understands people—especially classmates—which means Winnie has to untangle human relationships in the same way she listens to and gentles horses. In each story, God helps her in her spiritual journey and understanding.

Journal Entry—Within each story, Winnie writes to God, sometimes griping, sometimes thanking, sometimes asking for much-needed help. Journaling to God helps her slow her raging thoughts and emotions so she can be open and honest with Jesus.

Lassoing the Truth—This section helps make the connection between Winnie's story and your life. Watching Winnie grow through Scripture in each story can help you in your own faith journey as you apply the truth to your own life.

Whoa!—This is your opportunity to journal to God as Winnie does, getting real with Jesus. You can take your time writing how you feel, what's on your mind—anything. Pour out your heart and ask for help, or thank your heavenly Father for caring.

Prayer—Each devotional includes a prayer you can build on. Talk to God and pray about whatever is on your mind and heart.

Giddyup!—This verse activity is an opportunity to act on what you've learned and to remember God's Word forever.

Psalm 119:162 says, "I rejoice in your word like one who discovers a great treasure." Long ago, Winnie's mom made her a Treasure Box, filled with Scripture verses written on colored index cards. She told Winnie that the treasures, the verses, would encourage her and remind her of God's love wherever life took her.

You can make your own treasure cards. It's easy! You only need three things:

1. A pack of colored index cards with five colors. (You could also use colored construction paper or sticky notes, or you could use white cards or paper, color coding them with crayons or colored pencils.) Assign one card color for each category based on the emotions they address. For example:

   GREEN = HAPPY/JOYFUL
   RED = ANGRY
   BLUE = SAD
   YELLOW = CONFUSED
   PURPLE = SCARED/ANXIOUS

2. Something to write with (a pen, pencil, fine marker, etc.).

3. A special place to keep the cards. You could use a shoebox, gift box, recipe box, or file box. If you're stuck on getting a box, you can punch the top left corner of the cards and add a key ring or tie them together by color.

At the end of each devotion, the Giddyup! section will show you how to make and fill your box of treasures. By the end of the book, you'll have a box full of treasure cards to keep with you wherever you go.

1

Listen!

[Jesus] added, "Pay close attention to what you hear. The closer you listen, the more understanding you will be given—and you will receive even more."

Mark 4:24

Here's what's been on my mind: Mom, as usual. For the multi-millionth time, I thank God for making my mother the best horse gentler in the whole world. I remember how she used praise, patience, kindness, and firmness to gentle even angry stallions. I never saw her punish a horse or break his spirit, like most trainers did. Horses listened to Mom the way she listened to them.

I want to be a great horse gentler like Mom was, but what if I can't be?

I step into a gray morning that fits my mood. I'm grateful people keep bringing me their problem horses. But it's been a while since I've faced off with a Mustang like the one I'm waiting for. The Ohio Horse Rescue called me after Spidell's Stable-Mart refused to take a wild Mustang into their fancy stable.

I hear an angry whinny before I see the truck pull up. A wiry guy hops out of the cab looking as pleased to be here as that Mustang sounds. I jog to meet him. "Hey!"

He flicks his bangs away from his eyes. "Somebody expecting a Mustang?"

"Me. I'm Winnie." I don't add "the Horse Gentler."

"Winnie Willis?" He looks past me, then shrugs. "Sign this." I do, and he wrestles the little Mustang down the ramp. "Sam's all yours." He hands me the rope, and I barely get out of the way before he drives off.

"Welcome . . . Sam?" He's shaggy, with too-wide brown eyes. When I try to scratch his chest, he backs away. "That's okay," I lie. Finding a horse's scratching spot can make gentling easier.

I want to get started, but Sam needs to get used to his new home. I've kept the other horses in the barn, but it's still not easy leading him to the pasture. I breathe in the amazing scent of horse and grass. "Sam, wait till you meet Nickers, the sweetest horse in the world."

When I unhook the Mustang, he tears off galloping like his tail's on fire. I watch the restless Mustang race the fence as if scouting for a way out.

"Groovy little horse."

"Catman!" Calvin "Catman" Coolidge, probably my best friend in the world, could sneak up on a bat. He's a throwback to the hippies—long blond hair, striped bell-bottoms, tie-dyed T-shirt with a peace symbol. Cats swarm around his flip-flops. My little sister, Lizzy, calls him the Pied Piper of Cats.

He nods toward Sam, asking without words why I'm here and Sam's there.

"I'm letting him get used to things, but he needs to get used to me." I shout to the far end of the pasture. "Here, Sam!"

"Is he deaf?" Catman has helped me long enough to know better.

Hiding the leadrope behind me, I keep talking, narrowing the distance between Sam and me. "I just want to groom you, Sam." I pretend I'm trying to catch an invisible horse. I get close, but Sam jerks away. "Catman, let Nickers out." In seconds, my gorgeous white Arabian gallops up to me and slides to a stop. I pretend I'm catching Nickers, then reach over and snap the leadrope onto Sam's halter.

Things get worse inside the round pen. Catman and our buddy M helped me build it, just like Mom's in Wyoming. Sam is not impressed.

"Move out!" I command from the center of the pen.

No! Sam says, holding his ground. The point is to get the Mustang to walk or trot around the circle while I hold the long lunge line from the center. I step closer, arms raised. Sam stays put.

Finally, when I flick the line behind him, Sam takes a dozen steps.

"Far out!" Catman claps without a sound.

I feel like cheering too . . . until Sam stops. Nothing will make him move. Growing more and more frustrated, I shout, "Sam, GO!" Sam doesn't listen or care. I'm out of patience and getting angry. I know when to quit.

When Catman leaves, I groom Sam and turn him out to pasture without a word. Why bother when he wouldn't listen anyway? I watch the little horse slink off, head hung low like he doesn't have a friend in the world . . . or a mother. And I feel awful. Rotten. Sorry.

After supper, I pull out my Treasure Box. Mom gave it to me the day before my birthday, the day of the accident. She'd filled it with colored cards: Green = Happy/Joyful; Red = Angry; Blue = Sad; Yellow = Confused; Purple = Scared/Anxious. Mom wrote Bible verses on each card and said God wrote every word inside the box, and I should always listen to God's Word.

Since I'm confused about what to do with Sam, I pull a yellow card from the box:

Pay close attention to what you hear. The closer you listen, the more understanding you will be given—and you will receive even more.

Mark 4:24

I chew on that verse for a minute. I got frustrated with Sam today for not listening. But I guess I wasn't listening to God.

I pull out my journal and pour out my heart to God.

Dear God,

I guess it's silly to write since you know my thoughts before I do. But it slows me down so I can sort out what I'm struggling to understand. It feels like talking to you, which is what Mom called prayer.

I'm sorry for today. I didn't ask for your help, not even once. You created Sam, and I should have listened for you to guide me.

Please help me listen to you tomorrow. Thanks for always listening to me.

Love, Winnie

To be continued . . .

Lassoing the Truth

In this story, Winnie wanted Sam the Mustang to listen to her, and her patience grew thin when that didn't happen. Later, Winnie realized that she hadn't been listening to God or asking for God's help with the Mustang. In the same way, it can be easy to forget to ask God for help and direction, especially when something is bothering us. Is something bothering you? Take time to ask God for his wisdom—and really listen for his answer.

Whoa!

What are some ways you listen to God? (Read Scripture? Talk to a friend? Take a walk and talk honestly with God?) How could you focus more on listening to God? Slow down and journal to your heavenly Father about your desire to listen to him more.

____

____

____

____

____

____

____

Father, thank you for wanting a close relationship with me. I want that too. Please help me listen to you. And thanks for always listening to me.

Giddyup!

Start your Treasure Box! Make sure you have your cards, pens, and a box to store the finished cards in. (Take a look at pages xiv–xv for full instructions.) Copy today's verse onto a yellow card.

Pay close attention to what you hear. The closer you listen, the more understanding you will be given—and you will receive even more.

Mark 4:24

2

Present!

I will never leave you; I will always be by your side.

Hebrews 13:5, The Voice

I wake with a jerk that shakes my bed. I think I had a nightmare about Sam the Mustang. Lizzy's voice floats in from her room. She's talking to God the way she does. For a while, I stay in bed and listen to her happiness (although I can't make out the words).

I bring out my Treasure Box because I'll need all the help I can get for gentling Sam. I choose a purple card, hoping for peace and joy:

I will never leave you, Winnie; I will always be by your side.
Hebrews 13:5

Sometimes Mom stuck in my name, but it's not in the real verse. I want to run to the pasture for another chance with Sam, but I need to journal to God first.

Dear God,

Thank you for this promise, especially now. On my own, I don't think I can gentle Sam the Mustang. Yesterday I forgot that you were on my side. I didn't ask for your help. And I wasn't listening for you. Please help me gentle Sam today.

Love, Winnie

After breaking the Olympic record for Getting Dressed Fast, I race to the kitchen, hug my little sister, grab a peanut butter biscuit, and jog to the pasture. The sun is pushing off the horizon into a blue sky. Nickers and I exchange a horse-to-horse greeting. I blow into her nostril, and she returns the favor. When I first met Nickers, she'd been dubbed Wild Thing, and she deserved the name. God and I weren't talking much then. Or at least, I wasn't listening. But he gave me the best-ever gift anyway.

Remembering that God is by my side, I stop rushing and allow myself a short ride on Nickers. Skipping bridle and saddle, I use my legs to guide us to the woods. Wind tugs my hair as I hold onto Nickers's silky white mane. I feel closest to God at moments like this, as if trees and skies are laughing for joy and God's arms wrap around Nickers and me.

I could ride Nickers forever, but my thoughts start

turning to Sam—not worrying, but ready for Sam the Mustang.

I walk to the Mustang, and Sam's snort and wide eyes say he'd rather eat snakes than do battle with me again. He backs away from me. I stay calm and keep smiling, picturing Jesus smiling with me. "Sam, I'm sorry about yesterday. I wasn't listening to you or to Jesus, who's already forgiven me."

Sam's ears flick, a sign that he's paying attention.

Without planning it, I begin singing that hymn I love about amazing grace. My voice sounds like a cow-and-angry-stallion duet. But I'll bet that thought and song came from Jesus. Sam holds still while I put on his halter and leadrope. Then, still singing, I scratch him until I find his sweet spot, the special area God builds into each horse, where that horse loves to be scratched. Soon as I reach under Sam's mane, his muscles relax and his stiff ears flick up and back.

"Groovy!" Catman appears out of nowhere, a parade of cats at his heels. He walks right up to Sam and scratches under his mane.

"Catman, thanks for coming. Sam and I are heading to the round pen."

He turns to Sam. "Follow me, Samuel." And Sam does.

In the round pen, I put Sam on the long lunge line, and I move to the center of the ring. If I thought listening to God would work like magic, I was wrong. Yesterday's problems are still here. I give the command "Move out!" but Sam's legs stay planted. I move behind him and give the signal. He ignores it. My grip tightens on the rope. I try again and again, and my voice sounds sharper. "Catman, why won't Sam listen?"

Catman's gaze shifts between Sam and me. "Deep."

So I ask God. *I know you're here, but I need to hear you.*

Of course, I'm here! Didn't I promise I'd always be by your side and never leave?

I knew it! You calmed me down when I started losing patience again. Right? And–

Catman is staring inches from my face. "Are you talking to God?"

I nod.

"Far out! Is God talking back?"

My friend is totally serious, so I try to give him a serious answer. "I believe Jesus is with me, but I need to know it for myself."

His eyebrows are question marks. I'm not sure that made sense, even to me. "Remember how Ms. Pento called roll call, and I had to answer, 'Present!' even though she saw me on the front row and knew I was there?"

Catman nods.

"I know God's here, but I want him to say, 'Present.' Then when I really listen, I can hear him, just not with words." I glance up, embarrassed I said that out loud. But I see in Catman's eyes he gets it. "I only hear him inside my head, or heart, but it's enough."

We work the rest of the day, and Sam slowly understands the "Move out" command. Twice, he trots around the pen and only stops on cue–when I step toward his nose and say, "Whoa." It doesn't work every time, but it's an answer. I heard it.

Lassoing the Truth

When Winnie remembered that Jesus would be with her, gentling the Mustang took on a new perspective. She relaxed and listened to God, thinking of pieces of Scripture and God's promise to always be with her. Like Winnie in this story, we can forget that Jesus is present and ready to help. If you're struggling with a problem, stop and sense God's presence. Thank him that he will never leave, no matter what.

Whoa!

Journal about your friendship with God. Does he ever feel far away? Does he sometimes feel close by? Write about those times. What are some ways God has let you know he is close beside you?

____

____

____

____

____

____

____

Dear God, thank you for ALWAYS being with me wherever I am and no matter how I feel. Help me realize the gift of your presence all day long.

Giddyup!

Copy today's verse onto a purple card, sticking in your name where Winnie's appeared.

I will never leave you, __________ ;
I will always be by your side.
Hebrews 13:5, THE VOICE

You can memorize the promise by repeating it several times during the day.

3 Families

God places the lonely in families.

Psalm 68:6

This is the third time this week that I'm home alone. Dad is off inventing a phone hat with his "friend" Madeline. Lizzy's sleeping over at Geri's *again*. When I woke up in my silent house, I chose a blue card from my Treasure Box:

God places the lonely in families.
Psalm 68:6

So how come I'm feeling left out of mine?

I trudge out to exercise the boarding horses. By the time I get to ride Nickers, the humidity turns her so sweaty I cut our ride short. I should write in my journal, but I'm too busy feeling sorry for myself.

"MEOW, MEOW!"

It's Catman's back bike! Dad invented a backwards bike, where you have to pedal backwards to go forward. Mine whinnies.

I grab my bike and race outside. Catman and I exchange greetings, but just with our eyes. If Catman were a horse, he'd be a good-natured Clydesdale. "Let's split," I say. I can speak Catman.

He grins, and we pedal backwards in unison for his house, Coolidge Castle. My mind camera flashes me a picture of the first time I saw Catman. It sure wasn't "like at first sight." He just showed up in our barn with a dozen cats swarming at his feet. He looked like hippies on TV—tall and lean, wavy blond hair in a ponytail longer than mine. Wire-rimmed glasses couldn't hide his intense blue eyes. He wore bell-bottoms and a funky sweatshirt with a peace sign on the back. Gazing around the barn, he shouted, "Outta sight!"

Coolidge Castle looks more like a haunted house. Gables stick up from the roof in odd directions as if blown by storms. Weeds are encouraged to cover the lawn, except for a mown strip for lawn ornaments. Last week's Wizard of Oz gnomes (Tin Man, Cowardly Lion, Scarecrow, and Dorothy) are now wearing turkey costumes, even though Thanksgiving is months away.

As if reading my mind, Catman says, "Bart and Claire love Thanksgiving." When he's around his parents, he does call them Mom and Dad.

We make our way inside, stepping over cats and back in time. Antiques and wall tapestries, red velvet curtains and matching love seats decorate the gym-sized living room. Cats scurry to greet us. I recognize Churchill, Wilhelm (whose name changed to Wilhelmina when she had kittens), and Cat Burglar ("Burg," white with a black mask).

"Calvin?" This has to be his mom, because no one else calls him that. Mrs. Coolidge's hair is wrapped around soup cans, and her fuzzy green slippers match her eyes. When she sees me, her hands fly out of the pockets of her orange robe. "Winnie!" She races to me and runs her fingers through my tangled hair. "Don't you ever dare cut these gorgeous locks!" She is the only human who likes my wild Mustang hair. "You're just in time, dear!"

I glance to Catman, and he whispers, "Contests."

The three of us fill out contest entries at the wobbly kitchen table. Mostly we laugh and snack. I always feel like I can ask Mrs. Coolidge anything. "Catman says you guys make more money from contests than from Smart Bart's Used Cars and Claire's Beauty Salon combined."

"Right as always!" She signs an entry to win another toaster—I see three on her counter. "Remember when we won a trip to Cairo, Milan, Russia, Dublin, Antwerp, Oxford, Warsaw, Rome, and so many others?"

"Yep." I also remember the trip took under a week. All towns are in Ohio.

The front door slams open, and in comes "Smart Bart." He's short and Volkswagen-shaped, sporting a hairpiece and a red Tweety Bird tie. "Say-ay-ay!" He launches into a joke. "What did the driver say when he walked into a German car dealership?"

I shake my head. I've probably heard it before, but I'm always laughing too hard to catch the punch line.

"'. . . sauerkraut!' I've got a million of 'em!" Smart Bart's laugh comes in huffs and sounds a bit like neighs.

Note to self: *I may never know the punch line.*

In the evening, we play a game that I'm sure either Catman or his dad made up. It's impossible to figure out the rules. So when it's my turn, I simply put down any card in my hand, and they go nuts and shout, "Beginner's luck!" They reward me with a toaster.

It's nearly dark when I leave. Catman comes with me and walks my bike so I can carry the toaster. I'm thinking that I'm not lonely now. Note to self: *What would it feel like to have a family like the Coolidges?* Then, before I can envy Catman, I realize I do have their family, on loan today.

"Catman, my Treasure Verse said God places the lonely in families. I think today he placed me in yours."

"Neat-O," he agrees. "Righteous. And anytime."

I walk into my house and smell a Lizzy creative dinner she must have left for us. It makes me smile inside. Light seeps under the basement door, where a pounding followed by "Yeow!" signals that Dad is inventing.

Home sweet home. Time to journal:

Dear God,

Thanks for letting me borrow Catman's family today. And thank you for placing me in my own family. That's a winning combination if you ask me—even better than winning a toaster.

Love, Winnie the Winner

Lassoing the Truth

Winnie felt lonely when her family members had their own things to do, but instead of letting envy ruin her day, she chose to be thankful for Catman's family as well as her own. Have you ever felt left out? You can fight envy by finding ways to be thankful.

Whoa!

What's your relationship like with each member of your family? Are there other people God has placed in your life who can be like family at times? Journal about these special people.

Dear God, thank you for my family and for those who feel like family.

Copy today's Bible verse onto a blue card.

God places the lonely in families.
Psalm 68:6

Talk to a friend or family member about what you think this verse means.

4

Herds

Your righteousness is like the mighty mountains, your justice like the ocean depths. You care for people and animals alike, O Lord.

Psalm 36:6

Mom used to say, "Winnie, in the beginning God created heaven and earth and horses, and sometimes I have to wonder if the good Lord should have quit while he was ahead." It was true when we—mostly Mom—were gentling horses (not breaking horses) at our Willis Wyoming Ranch. It's still true here, where Dad has settled my little sister, Lizzy, and me in Ashland, Ohio, after trying out the *I* states. (We went to school for a few months in Idaho, Iowa, Illinois, and Indiana.)

I have never liked the first day of a new school year. Or many of the other days either. The only way Ashland Middle School makes any sense at all is to think about horses. Horses, unlike people, make sense. I am an orphan filly thrown among herds ranging from rodeo broncos to Five-Gaited Saddle Horses, with a few Mustangs thrown in.

Summer Spidell and the cool kids—a herd of high-strung Thoroughbreds and American Saddle Horses—laugh just outside the school doors as if they're deciding who may enter. I enter anyway.

"You okay, Winnie?" Lizzy stares down at me, and I lie with a nod. A year younger and two inches taller, my sister is the nicest person on earth. We both got Mom's eyes and brown hair, but Lizzy's hair always looks perfect. She's the most popular person in her class but doesn't know it or care. Mom used to say if Lizzy were a horse, she'd be a Trakehner because they do everything well. I'd be a wild Mustang. Lizzy hoists her pack higher and says, "I should go to class."

I send her on her way, and I head for my classroom.

"Winnie!" Eddy Barker waves from his herd of athletic Quarter Horses, sporty but not stuck-up. He points to a desk next to him, one of the nicest things anybody has ever done.

"How are your brothers?" I slide in. "And their dogs?" Barker trained five dogs for his five brothers.

Before he can answer, our homeroom teacher interrupts with a thousand rules of school. Note to self: *It feels unfair that you can't run in the halls but get busted for being late to class.*

The room has already filled with competing herds. In the wild, horses join herds for protection or power. What I'm observing feels a lot like that. Summer's group has taken over the back row. I hear giggles and forced laughs. Every herd has a dominant mare who bosses the rest of the mares and always gets first dibs on everything. Summer Spidell is definitely the dominant mare. Her dad owns Spidell's Stable-Mart and admits fancy horses only.

The rest of the day, I observe herds in every classroom. At lunch they hover together and whisper about inferior herds. But when a cute guy passes, girls are no longer girlfriends. They're mares turning on other mares to win the attention of an incoming stallion.

By the time the buzzer sounds to set us free, I'm ready to test the no-running-in-the-hall rule before I'm trampled by the giant herd.

"How was your day?" Lizzy asks once I make it to the bus. She leaves her seat up front, where a dozen kids fought to sit with her, and plops next to me in back.

"Let's just say I can't wait to return to my own herd."

Once home, I race to the pasture for a ride. My amazing Arabian lifts her head and nickers, which is the sweetest sound in the universe and happens to be my mare's name. Everything inside me shouts, *Thank you, God, for Nickers!*

Nickers and I take the dirt path through the woods to the flatland, where we gallop full speed, wrapped in the wonder of creation. The scent of walnuts, cut grass, apples, and horse rises like incense.

When we trot back, the sun hangs low in purple clouds. Lizzy has supper on the table, tuna wraps made with bread and anonymous things. Dad takes three minutes to eat, then heads to the basement to invent a crate shower for dogs who hate baths.

I'm so beat that after doing dishes, I climb the stairs to my bedroom and pull out my Treasure Box from under the bed. Since I'm still anxious about school, I choose a purple card.

Your righteousness is like the mighty mountains,
your justice like the ocean depths. You care
for people and animals alike, O LORD.

Psalm 36:6

I open my window, hoping to hear the horses, then settle down with my journal.

Dear God,

What a day! Thanks for the nudge to care about people. Mom was right about this Treasure Box. She said I was going to have all these emotions for the rest of my life because you created us with a yearning for heaven, and earth is not heaven. But she said these verses could help me navigate through school, through life, and to eternity.

Lord, I know you're telling me I need to care for animals AND people. I've got the animal part down. But people? Not so much. Should be an interesting year.

Love, Winnie

Lassoing the Truth

Winnie knows how horses behave in herds, but she feels clueless when it comes to figuring out people, especially classmates. Yet God told Winnie to care about people. Most of us have had trouble with certain people who don't seem to care about us. If you ever feel that way, God can still call you to be the one to care. You can always ask for God's compassion for yourself and for other people.

Whoa!

Are there "herds" or groups at your school? Where do you fit in, and where don't you feel welcome? In your journal space below, describe what it feels like to be accepted or rejected. Ask God to help you care about someone who doesn't seem to care for you. Then journal a thank-you to God, who loves you unconditionally and cares deeply for you.

____

____

____

____

____

____

____

Dear God, please help me understand my classmates and others I just don't get. Help me to care for them.

Giddyup!

Copy today's Bible verse onto a purple card.

> Your righteousness is like the mighty mountains, your justice like the ocean depths. You care for people and animals alike, O Lord.
>
> Psalm 36:6

Pick someone you haven't been getting along with and begin asking God to help you care about that person.

5

Odd Girl Out

God decided in advance to adopt us into his own family by bringing us to himself through Jesus Christ. This is what he wanted to do, and it gave him great pleasure.

Ephesians 1:5

Second week of school, and everything there keeps getting worse. Why don't I fit in anywhere? It's not just that I don't belong in the popular group. I don't fit into any group. I am a Western saddle on a Thoroughbred racehorse.

My best friend, Catman Coolidge, has to eat with high schoolers this year, except on Fridays. This morning I spotted half a dozen cats in the bushes waiting for him, but no Catman, not even at lunch. Same goes for M.

Sometimes I eat at Eddy Barker's table, so the first thing I do in the cafeteria is conduct a search for him. When I find him, he's at a full table laughing with guys from his football team. There's nothing to do but head for the girls' table, which is easy to find because they already sound like chickens cackling.

Summer Spidell is the only girl who turns around to me. Besides Spidell's Stable-Mart, the Spidells own half of Ashland, and Summer thinks she's the queen. If she were a horse (something she'd never be), she'd be a pale-yellow American Saddle Horse—colorless, see-through personality, and high-strung. I used to muck stalls for Stable-Mart. Dad still does odd jobs there. So she believes Dad and I are her subjects and lowly servants.

"No room here, Winnie," Summer warns. "Sorry," she lies. I frown at the three empty seats at her table, so she adds, "You wouldn't like it here anyway. We're talking about makeup."

"And boys!" Hilary chimes in.

"Not horses," Sal, one of Summer's fans, explains. Sal is sometimes my friend too, only not today apparently.

This turns the chickens into hyenas. I think the whole lunchroom—maybe the whole entire school—is staring at me.

I eat my peanut butter sandwich alone and spend recess pretending to correct all the math problems I missed on our quiz.

The minute I get home from school, I drop off my books and race to the pasture. Nickers gallops to me, showing off her long, wavy mane with a twist of her neck. "I missed you too, Nickers," I whisper. Dark clouds have thickened, threatening a storm tonight. "Don't worry. You're safe in your stall, and I'll give you guys extra hay to keep you busy. For now, we both need a quick ride, don't you think?"

I know my horse agrees, and we set out for a pleasure ride, not wandering too far from home. When we're done, I groom Towaco, my sometimes-friend Hawk's Appaloosa; then Buddy, the yearling; and "Mustang Ma'am," the horse sent to me by the Ohio Horse Rescue when I returned Sam the Mustang all gentled for them.

Note to self: *Why can't I be part of a school herd the way I feel part of this horse herd?*

At dinner Lizzy thanks God for the spaghetti she made us. Then she adds, "Jesus, please help Winnie."

"Are you sick, Winnie?" Dad asks, searching for his fork, which is under his napkin.

"No. I'm fine." It isn't a total lie, because I'm not sick.

I announce that I'm going to bed early. Lizzy and I shared my bedroom until this year, when Lizzy chose to occupy the storage closet off the kitchen, claiming I snore and talk in my sleep. I do. I offered to be the one to move. The closet room is actually bigger than the bedroom, with shelves on two long walls. But Lizzy loves the shelves for her aquariums and other creatures. Plus, she's our official creative cook and likes being close to the kitchen.

I admit I miss having her here at night.

I sit at my little table by the window and open my journal.

Dear God,

I have to ask why you made me like this . . . and Summer and her posse like that?

Today at school I knew you were with me, and I appreciated that since I don't fit in with anybody else. Does it ever feel like you don't fit in either?

Lord, I'm going to pull out my Treasure Box and take a blue card because I am blue. Would you please talk to me through that verse? I know you always do, but sometimes it feels like I should have picked a different verse or I don't understand what you're saying. I know this isn't magic, but Mom said every word is from you, even if I don't get it. Okay—here goes:

God decided in advance to adopt us into his own family by bringing us to himself through Jesus Christ. This is what he wanted to do, and it gave him great pleasure.

Ephesians 1:5

Wow!

Thanks, Winnie

I put my Treasure Box away and gaze out my window. The horses must have chosen their stalls for the night, except for Nickers. A shaft of moonlight falls to the pasture, a spotlight on my Arabian. I stare at the moon, while soaking up God's creation and God's words. I am part of God's family, adopted into it because of Jesus. I'm a member of his herd!

Still taking that in, I slide under the covers and hug my pillow. I can't stop grinning and whisper, "Take that, world . . . and Summer Spidell. I'm in the best herd ever!"

Lassoing the Truth

At school, Winnie feels she doesn't fit into any of the "groups," or cliques. Only when she reads her Treasure Verse does she understand that she's in the best group possible: she's in God's family because of Jesus. If you ever feel left out, or like you don't fit, tell your heavenly Father. If you've trusted Christ, you are in the family of God. Herds don't get any better than that!

Whoa!

What does it mean to you to be part of God's family? Journal details of how God shows you that he accepts you and wants you in his herd. Thank him for delighting in you.

____

____

____

____

____

____

____

Dear God, thank you for adopting me into your family, the best herd ever!

Giddyup!

Add today's verse to a blue card for when you're blue because you've forgotten what a wonderful family you're part of.

God decided in advance to adopt us into his own family by bringing us to himself through Jesus Christ. This is what he wanted to do, and it gave him great pleasure.

Ephesians 1:5

As you go through the day, think about the fact that it gives God great pleasure to have you in his family through Christ.

6

Out of Sorts

[Love] does not demand its own way. It is not irritable, and it keeps no record of being wronged.

1 Corinthians 13:5

I've waited all week for Saturday, when Catman and I could go on a horse picnic to Oak Tree Field. Only when I find Nickers still in her stall, I know something's wrong, "What's up, girl?" I stroke her withers, then give her oats, but she doesn't respond or eat. Doc Stutzman, our vet, is out of town. What would I say to him anyway?

I feed the other horses before jogging to the house to call Catman. Then I head to the basement to find Dad. From the top step I hear laughter. I stop, knowing I'll find Madeline Edison down there. She's an inventor who makes money at it and has started spending a lot of time around Dad. I guess she's okay. I just wish she'd be okay somewhere else.

I start down the stairs. Madeline is leaning over Dad's

shoulder. Dad is blow-torching a rod for his dog-vater invention, a dog elevator.

Madeline whispers to Dad. If she were a horse, she'd be an untrained, eighteen-hands-high, American Saddle Horse.

"Dad!" I shout. He turns off the torch. "Something's wrong with Nickers."

"Hi, Winnie! Lunch ready?"

It's no use. "No." I bound up the stairs. *Why does she have to come?*

Lizzy appears with a jar of pickles. She has the table set for lunch—for four. "Hey, Winnie! Do you think Madeline will like egg-and-tuna sandwiches?"

All I can say to my sweet and creative-cooking sister is "Right." The rest is shouting inside my head.

Lizzy pulls her egg-and-tuna sandwiches from the fridge when Madeline and Dad come up. Dad makes me sit at the table with them. I eat, but I can't get in a word to Dad, so I stop trying. Madeline talks too much. When she puts her hand on Dad's arm, I leave the table to check on Nickers.

I find my horse standing in her stall. She acts like she doesn't even know me. I sit with her, wishing she'd eat the hay in her trough. Even that feels like Madeline's fault.

"Are you okay?" Lizzy appears, keeping about three horse lengths away.

Note to self: *How can someone who snuggles snakes and loves lizards be afraid of horses?* "What do you want, Lizzy?"

"Dad said to tell you to come in and hear about Madeline's new invention. But I came because I'm worried about you. You're out of sorts."

I feel the words like pinpricks in my soul. Mom used to say I was out of sorts when I got irritated like I am now, edgy and prickly. "Tell Dad Nickers needs me."

When I don't look at her, Lizzy leaves. But I hear her say, "Jesus, please show Winnie what's bothering her . . . and her horse."

I take Nickers to the cross ties for grooming, and there's Catman waiting, brush in hand.

"Why are you here? The picnic's canceled." I don't know why I'm upset with him. Nickers tosses her head, and I can barely snap her into the cross ties. I'm so frustrated I could cry.

Catman holds up a hoof pick. I grab it without a thank-you and start on Nickers's front hooves. When I pick up the back left leg, Nickers jerks her hoof down, something she hasn't done since people called her Wild Thing. I try again, dragging the pick around her horseshoe and cleaning mud from the frog, the V-shaped tissue in the center that absorbs shocks and helps blood flow. No sign of thrush or canker infection.

I'm putting the hoof back down when Catman points to it. "What's that?"

"What?" I snap. A speck of white flickers from the frog. "Easy, Nickers." I dig out a rock half the size of my pinkie fingernail. "That can't be what put Nickers out of sorts." But when I finish, she nudges me like the real Nickers. When I set her free, she races to the pasture.

Catman's grinning, and I feel rotten for taking out my frustration on him. "Sorry, Catman. Maybe I have a rock in my foot too."

He helps me with barn chores, and we plot our next horse picnic before he has to leave.

Finished with chores, I sneak up to my bedroom, but Lizzy catches me. "Winnie, Dad says you need to come down and say goodbye to Madeline."

"Tell him I need to write in my journal."

Lizzy leaves, and I hear her say, "Please help Winnie."

I left my journal open on my bed. I sit next to it and start to write.

Dear God,

Lizzy is right. I do need help. I'm glad Nickers feels better, and thanks, because I'm sure you had a lot to do with that. But I'm still out of sorts. I haven't read a Treasure Verse today, so I'll do that now and be right back.

I pull out a red card.

[Love] does not demand its own way. It is not irritable, and it keeps no record of being wronged.

1 Corinthians 13:5

Lord, wow! "Demanding its own way"—check. "Irritable"—check. "Keeping a record of being wronged"—check. I've been hanging on to everything I don't like about Madeline. I don't want her here. I want Mom. I've kept a record of every time she gets between Dad and me, every little thing she does that irritates me. She shows up, and it feels like a stone inside me.

Heavenly Father, I need your love to wash my stone away. Thanks for forgiving me. I guess I need that love to reach Madeline too. Could you help me stop resenting her for seeing so much of Dad? Good thing nothing is impossible with you!

I'm signing off now. Guess I better go tell Madeline goodbye.

Love, Winnie

Lassoing the Truth

Winnie felt irritable and out of sorts. Once she realized why she felt that way, she was able to ask for God's help in changing her attitude. In the same way, if you're feeling irritable and grouchy, you can ask God to help you understand why. Look to God for help, and study today's verse about not hanging on to every hurt and not demanding your own way.

Whoa!

Have you ever been out of sorts? What kinds of things make you irritable? Is anything acting like a tiny rock in your shoe now? Journal to God about what that feels like, and ask for help in taking out that rock.

Dear God, I'm sorry I get frustrated and out of sorts. Please help me realize when I have a "rock" irritating me, and help me get rid of it.

Giddyup!

Choose a color card for when you're out of sorts. Copy your Treasure Verse onto that color card.

[Love] does not demand its own way. It is not irritable, and it keeps no record of being wronged.
1 Corinthians 13:5

Memorize the verse, focusing on God's love for you.

7

Thanks for That?

Give thanks for everything to God the Father in the name of our Lord Jesus Christ.

Ephesians 5:20

I woke up before the sun, so I have time to start the day with a Treasure Verse and still have time to journal. Since it's too early for me to have emotions, I pick a green card, going for happy.

Give thanks for everything to God the Father in the name of our Lord Jesus Christ.

Ephesians 5:20

Then I turn to my journal.

Dear God,

I understand I need to thank you more. Jesus' dying for us and coming back to life makes everything else possible. So, thanks for that! I'm always thankful for Nickers and Lizzy, and Dad most of the time.

But seriously, thanks for everything? Even bad stuff?

You said it, so I'll try it. I will do my best to give you thanks for everything today.

Love, Winnie

PS Thank you for the verse about thanking you!

I pull on "floor clothes," dirty jeans and a sweatshirt that should have gone into the laundry, and hurry to do barn chores before the bus comes. I'm greeted by gray skies and a cold drizzle. The sky looks like the inside of a giant stone. I thank God for it. Then I follow with heartfelt thanks for Nickers, Towaco, Buddy, and each horse I'm gentling.

When I finish graining the horses (giving Nickers an extra handful), I turn to go get ready for school, but I trip over a pitchfork I'd stuck in the hay. Down I go, taking a mound of hay with me. I'm all right, except for sneezing as I take the pitchfork to the tack room.

"Winnie, bus is here!" Lizzy cries.

No way. There's no time to change clothes. Yanking straw from my frizzy hair with one hand, I take my backpack from Lizzy, race for the bus, and leap through the bus doors. Lizzy tries to brush dirt and straw from my shirt and jeans, while I finger-comb my hair. "Lizzy, my barn boots!" They're a disaster even when clean.

When we give up on my dirty boots, I ask, "Lizzy, does the verse about thanking God for everything really mean *everything?*"

She yanks a piece of straw from my hair. "Yep. Sometimes it's easier than other times."

Note to self: *That pitchfork could have stabbed me—thanks that it didn't. The bus got here safely. I didn't stumble getting on and off.*

As the bus pulls up at school, I pray, *Thanks for Catman's cats waiting for him in the bushes, especially for Wilhelmina. Sure would be nice to see Catman.*

Note to self: *Ask Lizzy if I need to thank God for not seeing Catman.*

I grin inside when Ms. Brumby strolls into English class looking like an aggravated ghost, dressed head-to-high-heels in white, her color of the day, which happens to be the color of my horse. *Thanks that today's color can remind me of Nickers.* I really mean that.

I glance from Ms. Brumby's white heels to my brown boots. *Thanks for these boots?* I pray. Can't say I feel it, though.

The rest of the day I remind myself to give thanks, not just saying it, but giving it—like a well-deserved gift.

Sometimes it's natural: when Eddy Barker shouts across the hall that he loves my boots; when Catman and M save me a seat at lunch; when M entertains me by eating his sandwich in the shape of a cowboy boot; and when Catman says, "Groovy threads, Winnie!"

Other times my thank-you sounds forced, even inside my head: for Lizzy's sardine sandwich, for my sorta-friend Hawk ignoring me because she's sitting with Summer, for a glimpse of myself in the bathroom mirror.

Still, I'm about to thank God that I've made it through the day of thanks when I walk into my last hour study hall. Summer stops in the middle of the library and turns to me. She's wearing a silky, formfitting pink dress that I think I saw on the cover of *WOW Magazine* in the checkout lane. "What's that smell?" she says, loud as a mad stallion. She calls out to Mr. White, study hall monitor, and nods my way. "Isn't there a dress code this year, Mr. White?"

Lizzy and I walk home in a drizzle because I made us late for the bus. We don't say anything until we pass Brookside Park. "Lizzy, am I really supposed to give thanks for everything? I'm just not thankful for Summer or her herd."

Lizzy walks backwards so we're face-to-face. "That's what God tells us he wants."

"But I won't mean it."

"God knows that, Winnie. Like when you thanked me for the sardine lunch, I knew you didn't mean it, but it made me happy that you appreciated it. Maybe thanking God makes him happy. And that's really something—that little me could make the Creator of the Universe happy! Plus, sometimes, if you keep saying thanks even when you don't feel it, one day you may realize you do feel it, at least a little bit."

I think about that the rest of our muddy trek home. Twice I have to catch my sister when she slips in her gym shoes. *God, thank you for Lizzy.* All at once, I let out a horse laugh that makes Lizzy stop and stare at me. "Lizzy! Today I thanked God for my dirty boots, but now I mean it. I haven't slipped in the mud, not even once."

Lassoing the Truth

Winnie tried to thank God for everything, even though she didn't feel thankful. Lizzy helped her understand that she could make the Creator of the Universe happy by giving thanks no matter what. In the same way, we can share Christ's joy when we give him thanks. There is never a bad time or place to give God thanks!

Whoa!

What things are easy for you to give thanks for? What circumstances, or people, aren't so easy to be thankful for? Journal to God about people and situations that make it tough for you to be thankful. Thank God anyway.

Dear God, please remind me to give you thanks for everything in Christ's name.

Giddyup!

Copy today's verse onto whatever color card fits how you're feeling right now.

Give thanks for everything to God the Father
in the name of our Lord Jesus Christ.

Ephesians 5:20

Be on the lookout for opportunities to thank God for things you've never thanked him for.

8

Who's the Boss?

Work willingly at whatever you do, as though you were working for the Lord rather than for people.

Colossians 3:23

Math hates me!

I hate it back.

My math teacher, Ms. Akers, isn't crazy about me either. She probably dreaded grading my math test as much as I dreaded taking it. Almost. I wait until the last minute and slip into my seat in the back of her classroom. If Ms. Akers were a horse, she'd be an Akhal-Teke, a hot-blooded breed from Turkmenistan, where nomads needed a strong horse the owner could count on. God gave this breed a weird instinct, to develop strong bonds with one single rider and consider other humans the enemy. The horse will kick or bite anyone she thinks threatens her friend.

Ms. Akers's friend is Summer Spidell.

I'm pretty friendly with Spanish, art, history, and English (most of the time).

Math thinks I'm the enemy. (Just ask Ms. Akers.)

"Most of you didn't fare as well on your exams as I'd hoped." Ms. Akers's pinched lips part into an actual smile as she hands back Summer's exam. "I see improvement in your efforts. Good for you, Summer!"

Wordlessly, our teacher plunks down graded exams on each desk before thundering to the back row, smile gone. She tosses my math test on my desk. "Winnie, you must study harder. I want you to review the basics—multiplication and division, even addition and subtraction."

I nod.

Note to self: *I'd just multiply my hate—sorry—my dislike of math and divide my brain into little pieces, adding to my troubles and subtracting all joy from life.*

I tell myself I don't care. At least it's Friday, the beginning of a math-free weekend.

I don't feel like riding the bus, so I walk home, my backpack weighed down by my extra-heavy math book. Lizzy is already at the kitchen table . . . studying. "Really, Lizzy? Studying on a Friday afternoon?"

My little sister smiles up at me as if she's studying a plateful of cookies instead of her history workbook. "I want to get studying out of the way. Geri's coming over tomorrow. She's going to help me find another blue-bellied fence lizard, and I'll help her search for frogs."

Note to self: *Ms. Akers will love Lizzy.*

Mom used to say, "When in doubt, Winnie, ride it out."

"I'm going for a ride," I inform my sister.

In a few minutes, Nickers and I are sailing with the

breeze, setting my mind free to talk with God. I breathe in the scent of wild mint and horse and move with the rhythm of Nickers's pounding hooves. *Lord, I don't think I'm lazy, like Ms. Akhal-Teke says. Didn't I work hard to get Sam the Mustang ready for a new owner? And I spent days getting Towaco ready for Hawk to ride. Pat relies on me at Pat's Pets because I always answer horse questions on the Pet Helpline. I read my chapters for history and science. So why should I do everything my math teacher tells me to when there's no way to please her?*

Note to self: *I am making pretty good sense here.*

When we finally return to the barn, I groom and cool off Nickers. After that, I exercise the new horse and feed the others, doling out fresh hay.

Lizzy has made "Lizard Stew," but I'm guessing she used last night's leftover chicken.

"It's good, Lizzy. Thanks." I know she worked hard on it. I turn to Dad, who's wearing his inventing clothes, a one-piece jumpsuit that looks like an astronaut suit. "Dad, do you like Lizzy's Lizard Stew?"

"I've always loved the taste of lizard," he says, totally serious . . . until he winks.

After doing dishes, I head for my room. But halfway there, I get a flashback of Ms. Akers telling me to study more. A Scripture verse is at the edge of my memory, something about working for a bad boss?

I search through my Treasure Box, checking red and blue and purple, but finally find it in green. Green = Happy. Mom thought studying was happy?

Work willingly at whatever you do, as though you were working for the Lord rather than for people.

Colossians 3:23

It's the verse I was looking for. I reread it, then take out my journal.

Dear God,

I had to read this verse three times before I really got it. I'm not working for math or for Ms. Akers, am I, Lord? I'm working for you. "Whatever you do" means whether I'm riding Nickers or training a Mustang . . . or learning math, YOU are my boss. Mom was right. Working for you makes angry red turn into happy green.

Thanks for being the Boss and never giving up on me.

Love, Winnie

I hurry to the kitchen and pull out my math book from my backpack. Dad has rubber bands, screws, and lids spread across the kitchen table for a new invention. So I start back to my room.

"Winnie? Is that your math book? You're not studying on a Friday night, are you?" Dad's eyes are wide in shock, making me laugh. He laughs too.

"Yep. Gotta work hard for the Boss, Dad."

He clears me a book-sized spot on the table. "Go for it, if you're sure you're feeling all right."

I picture Jesus smiling at both of us. "I'm feeling great, Dad. Time to get to work." True, I'd rather work on anything other than math. But then, I'm not the Boss.

Lassoing the Truth

Winnie doesn't like math, partly because she isn't great at it. We all have weaknesses in schoolwork and in life. But understanding that we work for God can give us a new perspective, as it did Winnie in the story. If you're not happy with a teacher, a boss, a coach, or anyone telling you what to do, remember that whatever you have to do, you work for God. Give it all you got!

Whoa!

Do you have a class or activity that gives you trouble? Journal about those difficulties, and then ask for God's help. Thank him for being your "Boss." Write what it might look like to "work willingly at whatever you do, as though you were working for the Lord."

Dear God, I'm glad you're my boss. Please help me do the best work I can do.

Giddyup!

Choose your card color and copy today's verse.

Work willingly at whatever you do, as though you were working for the Lord rather than for people.

Colossians 3:23

Choose at least one chore, assignment, or goal, and work extra hard at it all week, picturing Jesus as your loving Boss.

9

Letdown

Most important of all, continue to show deep love for each other, for love covers a multitude of sins.

1 Peter 4:8

From backstage, I scan the rows of chairs set up in the school gym. Our whole entire class had to write a speech and say it in front of everybody. Our principal chose three kids to give their speeches tonight. And I'm one of those three! I'm almost never one of anything.

Barker is onstage giving his speech on how to choose the right pet for your family. It ends with "Get a dog." His mom, dad, granny, and great-granny, plus all five brothers take up the front row on the edge of their seats, smiles bursting until he finishes and they can cheer.

Lizzy waves from an aisle seat. Next to her is an empty seat, with no Dad in it.

I'm last. When I walk to the microphone, I can't help staring at the empty seat next to my sister. It looks bigger than other seats. I think the smell of gym sweat and cleaning stuff is making me queasy.

"Winnie?" Mr. Russell says, maybe for the third time.

"Horses are a lot like people," I begin, "only less selfish." When I gave my speech to our class, I was so excited about sharing the wonder of horses that I forgot to be nervous. I'm not nervous now, but that's because I'm too disappointed. The words come out without traveling through my brain.

After the gym empties, Lizzy and I catch a ride in the Barker Bus (a big, old van). The crowded passengers fill the van with praise for Eddy and me. Granny B. shouts, "Why, I want to go out and buy me a dog and a horse!"

"Thanks for the lift," Lizzy says as we climb out to a dark front lawn. Nobody turned on the front light, so we're careful not to trip over pipes, wires, car parts—junk Dad might need for inventions. "You did great!" Lizzy says as I stumble over a sink trying to reach our front door.

Dad's footsteps coming up from the basement match my heartbeat. At the top of the stairs, he asks, "Where've you two been so—?" He palm-smacks his forehead. "Your speech! Winnie, I'm so sorry. I've almost invented battery boots! Even if you can't dance, your boots will." His face drains of enthusiasm. "How did it go?"

"Winnie was awesome!" Lizzy's head swivels from Dad to me. "Winnie, tell Dad about your speech." I shake my head. She turns to Dad. "Dad, those boots sound great."

His face shines brighter than our front lawn with the light on. "I think this could be the one! The boots move from rock 'n' roll to waltz. And the batteries are rechargeable!"

I turn my back on him. "I'm going to bed." I run to my room, where I grab my journal and curl up in bed.

Dear God,

I know I should be thanking you for letting me be one of three. But I'm so let down by Dad. Couldn't he show up like other parents? Are dancing boots more important than a speaking daughter?

He forgets to pick up a notebook, or paints for school, or anything I ask for. We don't talk about Mom, and sometimes I think he's forgotten her.

I'm sorry I'm getting this journal wet, but something's in my eye. Heavenly Father, I wish you could talk to me and make it better. I know. Mom used to say the best way you talk to us is through the Bible. Guess it's time for a blue card from my Treasure Box.

Most important of all, continue to show deep love for each other, for love covers a multitude of sins.

1 Peter 4:8

I read the verse and finish journaling.

Lord, I don't feel like showing deep love or covering Dad's forgetting me, not paying attention to me, not caring. Sorry.

Love, Winnie

I try to fall asleep and forget about Dad like he forgets about me. But I can't. My mind replays the day Dad threw stuff in the truck, including Lizzy and me, and didn't tell us we were moving until we passed the highway sign: COME AGAIN. LOVE, WYOMING.

But I think God is still talking to me through my Treasure Verse. God's love covers all of *my* sins. Why do I keep replaying Dad's letdowns?

I know Dad loves me, even when I'm not feeling it. He doesn't even like horses, but he let me have Nickers and gentle horses. He loves Lizzy and me enough to muck stalls at Spidell's Stable-Mart.

I head for the basement but stop on the first step because Dad is staring into his wallet. Guess I'm not the only one short on cash. I take another step and see he's staring at a picture of Mom.

When Dad sees me, he snaps his wallet closed. "Winnie? I'm sorry I missed your speech. Your mom would have made sure we were in the front row."

"I know." A silence passes between us. I'm not sure what to say, but the mad is slowly leaking from me.

Dad keeps apologizing for tonight . . . and for other

letdowns I didn't think he thought about even when they happened. After the tenth time I tell him I'm over it . . . mostly, he asks, "Honey, are you sure you're okay?"

"I'm good, Dad." And I think I really am now, or will be. "Except for one thing: I want to try on those dancing boots."

Lassoing the Truth

When Winnie's dad let her down, she recalled other times he'd disappointed her, which made her angrier. But as she considered how God's love covered her own sins, she chose to love and forgive her dad. When *your* parents aren't perfect and let you down, like Winnie, you can choose to love deeply, as God loves you, and to forgive.

Whoa!

Have you ever been let down by someone? How did you respond? Journal to God about how you felt or feel. What would it feel like to forgive that person? Thank God for his deep love and for not keeping a record of your sins. If you're carrying a grudge from a disappointment, ask your heavenly Father to help you love and forgive.

Dear God, when people let me down, please help me understand and forgive, the way you always forgive me.

Giddyup!

Take a red or a blue card and write today's verse on it.

Most important of all, continue to show deep love for each other, for love covers a multitude of sins.
1 Peter 4:8

If you're holding a grudge against someone in your family, give him or her a hug. Don't be afraid to say, "I love you." If you have a grudge against someone else, try giving the person an unexpected encouragement or compliment.

10

Bad Mirrors

You made all the delicate, inner parts of my body and knit me together in my mother's womb. Thank you for making me so wonderfully complex! Your workmanship is marvelous—how well I know it.

Psalm 139:13-14

Before dashing off to school, I make a big mistake. I stop in front of my bedroom door and look. Last month Dad hung a full-length mirror on my door, a failed invention that was supposed to change from a regular mirror to a fun house mirror. I stare at my reflection and wish I could change my mirror to the fun house version. I'm not liking my real reflection.

I am a short, poorly dressed scarecrow. My hair is a churning brown ocean at high tide. I have ten times more freckles than my sister. At school I usually feel I look like a Mustang in a tornado. Thanks to this mirror, I see I'm right.

I barely make it to my first class when Kaylee slides into the chair next to me. "Winnie! I need to warn you. It's all they talk about!"

I'm clueless. "Who and what?"

My friend is dressed in an embroidered black tunic and stirrup pants. Her parents adopted her from China, and she has the most beautiful shiny black hair ever. "The Horse Show Princesses." Kaylee tips her head toward Summer and Hawk.

"I'll be happy to share the beauty secrets that made me Princess," Summer is saying. The popular mares squeal as if Summer is giving out keys to her kingdom.

"Didn't Harper and Madison get to be Queens of the Horse Show? Maybe we should ask them for secrets." I say this to Kaylee, but the steam coming from Summer's nose tells me I said it too loud.

Summer glares at me. "Take Winnie, for example—an example of what *not* to do. Hair is of primary importance, but hers is always wild and never styled. She can't help being too short, but she should wear decent shoes. A base cover-up and lipstick might do something to help her face."

Class is called to order, and it's the only time I'm glad for it. It's not so much that I'm embarrassed. What hurts is that Summer's right.

After school, I work on voice commands with the beautiful Friesian a father bought for his son. The mare does well, but my heart isn't in it. Same goes for the Quarter Horse gelding I'm getting ready for shows. I have time to ride Nickers but decide I need a Treasure Verse first. I keep hearing Summer's non-beauty tips in my head.

Back in my room, I finger through my Treasure Box and pick the blue card with the most words on it.

You made all the delicate, inner parts of my body and knit me together in my mother's womb. Thank you for making me so wonderfully complex! Your workmanship is marvelous—how well I know it.

Psalm 139:13-14

My mind is spinning too fast for my thoughts, so I pull out my journal and write to God.

Dear God,

I never thought about how you put me together in Mom's womb. I believe that you do wonderfully complex and marvelous workmanship, but I don't think I look wonderful or marvelous. And I sure don't feel that way.

I'm sorry. I know you always tell me the truth, so I have to believe it. But between you and me, I could use your help understanding.

Love, ~~Wonderful~~ Winnie

When I go back to the barn to groom Nickers, I brush her belly and think about Mom's womb with me inside. I imagine God knitting me together, attaching my bones to make me short but able to ride. Putting bones together sounds kind of cool, like playing with Legos or setting up the skeleton in biology lab.

I swing up on Nickers with echoes of Psalm 139 swirling in my odd-shaped head: *Wonderfully complex . . . Your workmanship is marvelous.*

Nickers and I canter on backroads covered with pine needles. Hoof music blends with whip-poor-wills and a pileated woodpecker. From somewhere comes the whiff of chimney smoke.

"Nickers, God's creation is 'wonderfully complex' and 'marvelous.'"

We slow walk by the McCray farm, and I take a good look at their gorgeous Standardbreds. I never noticed what a horse show judge would probably mark down. Hindquarters should be as full at the bottom as on top, but theirs aren't.

Back at the barn, after I turn Nickers out, I groom our boarder, an Appaloosa with the sweetest disposition. He has pretty good conformation, or structure. But an ideal horse should be as long as he is tall, and this horse is not. It doesn't matter. He's a great horse . . . and great-looking.

I fill the hay trough for the Friesian and admire his long mane and tail. He's muscular and pure black, with a white blaze. Most registries allow only a small star on the forehead for purebred registration, but I love his jagged blaze.

Even gorgeous Nickers might be faulted in a halter class

for measuring an inch short of "the perfect horse's" head-to-neck ratio.

"God made all of our parts. Horses too, Nickers. That makes us wonderful and marvelous."

That night, I face my mirror, surprised to see myself smiling. I'm still short, and my hair hasn't calmed down, but I think I'm okay. *God, thank you for knitting me in Mom's womb. You must have known what I'd look like. I admit it's not the way I would have done it, but you are the Creator Artist, and I am wonderfully made.*

Lassoing the Truth

Winnie didn't like the way she looked. But when she faced her Creator in her Treasure Verse, she felt better about herself. After all, God fashioned her in her mother's womb. Most of us have parts of our bodies we'd like to change. If you don't like something about the way you look, try seeing yourself through God's eyes. He thinks you're marvelous!

Whoa!

Explain to God how you feel when you look in the mirror. Take a good look and journal about the parts of your body you like and the parts you don't. Thank your Creator for making you his masterpiece!

Heavenly Father and Creator, help me trust that I'm marvelous in your eyes.

Giddyup!

Write today's verse on a blue card.

You made all the delicate, inner parts of my body and knit me together in my mother's womb. Thank you for making me so wonderfully complex! Your workmanship is marvelous—how well I know it.

Psalm 139:13-14

Pray for one of your classmates who might not feel "wonderfully complex" or "marvelous." Look for opportunities to observe something good about that person, and let her or him know.

11

Remembering

I recall all you have done, O LORD; I remember your wonderful deeds of long ago.

Psalm 77:11

Outside my window, the world is gray. Inside, I feel gray too. It's Saturday, and I always look forward to riding Nickers and training clients' horses.

Only not today.

Dear God,

I don't like the mind photos that have been popping up. My photographic memory would be great if I could pick which photos are snapped. But flashing through my mind all night were pictures of the accident: Dad's face when Mom and I left to pick up my birthday horse in spite of heavy snow; the trailer sliding; the telephone pole; rolling, crashing; Mom's head on the steering wheel . . . Note to self: Stop it!

Lord, it would be great if you would help me choose the right Treasure Verse. I'll pull an angry red card right now.

I recall all you have done, O LORD; I remember your wonderful deeds of long ago.
Psalm 77:11

It's a great verse, but not today. The last thing I need is to remember.

Thanks anyway, Winnie

Lancer, a sleek, long-legged bay, stops grazing when I enter the pasture. The old owner ran him in harness races, but the new owner bought him for trail rides. Lancer shies at everything, and his best gait is going *backwards.*

I'm leading Lancer to the barn when I see Catman. I wave, and Lancer jerks backwards, pulling the rope out of my hand, leaving me rope-burned.

Catman checks my hand. *What's that about?* his blue eyes silently ask.

I start to answer when M jogs up eating a Lizzy-made sandwich. I explain why Lancer ran off. "Poor horse has some bad memories of being mistreated. I can't get him to move past them."

Catman gives me his knowing look—he always knows. "Deep. Does Lancer have a photographic memory too?" He turns to M and explains, "Winnie's head flashes memory photos at her. Sometimes groovy. Not today."

M bends down to pick up Catman's long-haired cat, Aussie. "264," M says in a deep voice.

I don't get it. "264? Catman has a lot of cats, M, but 264?"

He grins. "That's how many times the Bible says, 'Remember'!"

M found Christ on Christmas Eve when a foal was born in our barn. The mother sacrificed herself to give birth to Buddy. M stayed with me to the end, and we had all night to talk about Jesus' birth and sacrifice. That night is filled with memories—some awful, some miraculous.

"Memories are tricky," I say, thinking out loud. "Bad ones are hard to get rid of. Lancer probably remembers being hurt or mistreated."

I glance at M to see if I've stirred up his bad memories. "You okay, M?" That night in the barn M told me social services took him out of his parents' home because they mistreated him.

"You've met the parents I adopted. My parents keep giving me good memories. The more good memories we make, the less room I have for bad ones." He holds up his sandwich, nibbled into a perfect cross.

I recall all you have done, O Lord; I remember your wonderful deeds. "That's it, you guys! We can give Lancer *good* memories!"

The rest of the day, M, Catman, and I play with Lancer. We roll balls and give him apples, handfuls of oats, and a couple of Lizzy's homemade horse treats. M hangs a hay-stuffed net from the stall's ceiling. Nickers joins in the fun. I lead Lancer, and Catman leads Nickers in tag, scattering leaves that whisper and crunch.

When we're all worn out, including Lancer, we groom both horses and turn them out together. "We have a long way to go," I admit. "But Lancer has some good memories now."

The sun touches the horizon as we sit wrapped in blankets to wait for stars.

"And you?" Catman asks, sitting crossed-legged next to me and my barn cat, Nelson.

"I have good memories," I answer. Then just like that, I get mind photos. "I can see every little line at the corners of Mom's eyes when she smiled at me. I see her crouched in a Wyoming bramblebush with me as we waited for Mustangs to come to the watering hole. I love the shot of Mom and Dad holding hands and surveying our Willis Wyoming Ranch—Dad in a three-piece suit he wore when he worked for the insurance company, Mom in jeans and a flannel shirt."

I also have a mental photo of the night Mom handed

me my Treasure Box. Only I'll keep that one to myself for now . . . unless Catman's reading my mind already.

Lizzy brings us paper plates of fish-s'ghetti. "It's snowing!" she cries.

We watch the tiny white flakes while God's golden ball slides down through puffy gray clouds. Shouts and laughter rise to greet the floating snowflakes. M pops up, then falls backwards, moving arms and legs as if making a snow angel in the lightly frosted dirt. Catman catches flakes on his tongue.

Thank you, my Father in heaven, for this moment. I laugh at Catman, who's trying to make a snowball out of melting flakes midair, and M's dirt angel, and Lizzy's curly hair sprinkled with snowflakes, and Nickers and Lancer kicking up from snowflake joy—as my mind flashes photos at the speed of light.

Lassoing the Truth

Throughout the Bible, God commands us to remember. But what if—like Winnie—we don't want to remember? Then we have to trust God to keep bad memories in the past—not blocked, but denied power to take over our thoughts. Then we can make wonderful new memories with Christ every day.

Whoa!

Write a prayer to God, turning your bad memories over to your loving Savior. Journal a few of your best memories. Ask God to help you create the best memories for the rest of your life.

Dear God, please help me remember all the great things you've done for me.

Giddyup!

On a blue or red card, write today's Treasure Verse.

I recall all you have done, O LORD; I remember your wonderful deeds of long ago.
Psalm 77:11

Pick out one great thing the Lord has done for you and share it with at least one person.

12

Change

Jesus Christ is the same yesterday, today, and forever.

Hebrews 13:8

Dear God,

Why can't everything stay the same?

Today Catman won't be riding his back bike to school with me like usual. He and M are in freshman science, and they're going in early to work on some experiment.

Lizzy just gave me two pairs of jeans because she's outgrown them. Shouldn't it be the other way around? And if I start writing about Dad's "friend" Madeline and how she's always taking Dad's time and attention away from Lizzy and me, I'll be here all day.

I don't have time to read a Treasure Verse now, but I'll take one with me. I better split, as Catman would say (if he were here, which he is not).

Sorry, Winnie

I pick a green card—not because I'm happy, but because I'd like to be—and shove it into my pocket. Of course, the weather changed overnight. No trace of snow. I don't even need a coat. When I park my bike in the school rack, I don't lock it, since who wants to pedal my Dad-invented bike backwards to go forward?

The buzzer sounds as I slide into my desk chair, which last week was next to Hawk. Only today, Hawk is in front next to Summer. Victoria "Hawk" Hawkins is so pretty with her black hair flowing to her waist that she gets paid for modeling. When I first gentled her Appaloosa, we got to be good friends.

That's changed. Now she's Summer's best friend.

After school, I wait for the halls to clear, then make my exit. A car whizzes by, but I turn in time to see Hawk's long black hair and Summer's blonde hair flying from Richard Spidell's convertible. *Changed* from his Land Rover.

On the steps, Catman is laughing with M and two other freshmen. I'd like to get Catman by himself and talk, but I don't know how. "Catman, I like your bell-bottoms with the orange flip-flops." I hardly ever comment on Catman's clothes, and I hope I don't sound as weird to him as I do to myself.

He turns to me with eyebrows raised and eyes

narrowed. "You like my threads, Winnie?" He gives me a second look, then says, "Lay it on me."

I do. He walks with me to the bike rack, and I tell him about Hawk and Summer, and Dad spending more time with Madeline, and Lizzy getting taller. "Everything is changing, Catman, even the weather. I don't like it."

He mounts his bike, and I'm waiting for his wise advice. "Bummer," he says.

"That's all you got?" I demand.

He locks me in his blue-eyed stare. "Heavy. Talk more tonight. I've gotta bug out."

Tonight is Moon Check night. Once a week, mostly, Catman meets me on our hill above the pasture for Moon Check. I count on that time for many reasons, one of which is talking with Catman.

Note to self: *Catman better never change.*

That evening Catman and I sit on our hill, ready to watch the sky show. M comes in time for sunset. The weakened ball of flames hides behind dapple-gray clouds, then drops fast as if swallowed by the horizon. The scent of pine, cold hay, and horse surrounds us. Nickers hangs close by.

M nibbles a candy bar in the shape of a question mark and holds it in front of Catman's face.

Catman mutters one word: "Change."

M nods as if he's just been given a lecture on what's wrong with Winnie.

"I know," I say. "I should be used to change by now, after Wyoming and the *I* states."

Lizzy joins us, carrying a tray of paper plates loaded

with "b's"—bread, bowls of barley soup, beets, beef, and beans. We thank her and scoot closer together on the blanket as we eat. Only munching, slurping, and chewing break the night's silence.

"Outta sight!" Catman points to the brightest star in the sky. He acts like he's never seen it before. "A hundred years from now, you could still use Polaris, the North Star, to find the direction north. It's more right-on than the best compass." He looks down to me. "That won't change."

"Wow!" Lizzy says, or prays. "Thank you for making that star and all the others."

M sits up straight and surprises me. "Amen!" he shouts. "All true. But even though the North Star doesn't seem to move, it does, a little. Still, the North Star is a symbol for never changing. Only God is never changing for real." He plops on his back and stares at the North Star. Nobody speaks. But M isn't done. "Polaris is a three-star, a triple-star system. They act as one—a superstar and two smaller stars—all bigger than our sun and 2,500 times brighter."

Lizzy says what I'm thinking: "Father, Son, Holy Spirit—Three-in-One."

"Yep. A symbol. It doesn't rise or set. It's just here," M says.

"Far out!" Catman and I say it at the same time. That never happens, and Lizzy can't stop laughing. It's contagious.

We grow quiet. An owl hoots from the woods, and wind whistles through pines. I hear a whinny and an answering whicker, a dog barking far away, a couple of Catman's cats purring.

Not until I go inside and get into my jammies do I pull my crumpled Treasure Verse from my pocket. I smooth it out and read:

Jesus Christ is the same yesterday, today, and forever.
Hebrews 13:8

I gaze out my window at the North Star, an amazing symbol far away. And I thank my way more amazing, *real* God, who made that star. Everything else may move and change, but I'll never be left on my own to face the changes. Jesus will be right here with me, *the same yesterday, today, and forever.*

Lassoing the Truth

Winnie wanted things to stay the same, but our Creator made a world with built-in changes—some we like, some we don't. When she understood that God never changes, that Jesus is the same yesterday, today, and tomorrow, peace followed with thanksgiving. When you face unwanted changes, you might experience sadness or fear. But you can remember that God never changes. He is the One you can always count on.

Whoa!

Are you going through any major changes right now? Or do you fear a change that might cloud your future? Journal honestly about your feelings. Then picture Jesus holding your hand, and write about how you can face, and even enjoy, earthly change, knowing that Jesus never changes.

____

____

____

____

____

____

____

Dear God, thank you for never changing! Help me trust you, no matter what changes around me.

Giddyup!

Write Hebrews 13:8 on a green or purple card—your choice.

Jesus Christ is the same yesterday, today, and forever.
Hebrews 13:8

Now, choose a color to match your emotion at this moment and write a second card for Malachi 3:6.

I am the LORD, and I do not change.
Malachi 3:6

Read each verse three times and thank God for never changing.

13

First Love

I have this against you, that you have left your first love.

Revelation 2:4, NASB

Dear God,

Sorry I haven't written to you lately. Things have been so busy. I've got to gentle two feisty ponies for Mrs. Fisher's two feisty grandsons. Plus, I've entered Nickers in the local horse show—the jumping competition and the Pleasure Horse class. I've ridden other people's horses in shows as part of their training, but this will be my first horse show with my own horse.

Gotta run! I'll have to read a verse later.

Winnie

After saddling Nickers with the English jump saddle Pat loaned me from Pat's Pets, I head toward the jumps at the far corner of the pasture. Nickers tries for the woods, where we usually go on long rides. "Not today, girl." She doesn't struggle, but I feel her disappointment. "Nickers, I really want us to win something, anything, in the horse show. Summer has a hundred trophies. All I want is one, or even a ribbon. Come on! Let's do this."

Neither of us enjoys practicing, but I make Nickers try the jumps I've set up.

M appears out of nowhere. "Having fun?" The way he asks says he knows the answer.

"The show's tomorrow, M, and Nickers still isn't clearing jumps." A gaggle of geese pass overhead, honking as if they're mocking, or maybe scolding, me.

M moves to stand by the poles he and Catman helped me set up to practice jumping. "Just in case you knock down the bar," he prophesies.

We do, three out of three tries. "I hate this," I mutter.

M silently urges me to try one more time.

"Okay." I squeeze my thighs, wondering if Nickers can feel the pressure through the saddle. She groans and then takes off and jumps so high the bar could have been on the top rung.

Catman runs up, shouting, "That was a blast! You were flying, man!"

"Catman! Did you see?" I'm still catching my breath. "She did it! Good girl, Nickers!"

Nickers sighs.

But what if she can't do it again? "We need more practice," I tell Catman and M.

I try the jump twelve times, and Nickers clears it only three times.

Catman whispers, "Mellow, Winnie."

I turn to M, and he's holding up a piece of toast nibbled into an octagon. It takes me a minute to recognize a toasted STOP sign.

Nickers agrees, planting her hooves where she stands. And honestly, I agree too.

After dinner, I take a long, hot bath like Mom used to do. When I come out, I realize I have not had fun riding my horse. How can that possibly be? My favorite thing in the whole world is riding Nickers.

I'm yearning for sleep, but I stumble over my Treasure Box on my way to bed. I start to kick it back under the bed. But I might as well pick a card—a yellow, confused card:

> I have this against you, that you have left your first love.
>
> Revelation 2:4, NASB

I think back through the last couple of weeks, the times I forgot to journal to God, days I didn't even think about Jesus. I didn't let God speak to me through the Bible because I didn't take time to read it.

I recover my journal, find a pen, and start to unravel the mess in my head.

Dear God,

Have I really lost my first love for you? I'm so sorry that I can't honestly answer that. I've skipped a lot of Treasure Verses and journaling, but that's not what you're saying, is it? Looking back this week and maybe before, I know my thoughts have been on that horse show, even more than on Nickers. Way more than my thoughts of you, Lord.

What a terrible loss for me to have lost my first love for you, my constant Friend, my Comfort and Peace, my Savior, Lord, Creator God! I've put that horse show trophy above desiring you, seeking it instead of you. Please forgive me. Thanks that you always forgive me because Jesus already paid for my sins.

Love, Winnie

"Thank you for loving me so much," I whisper. "You are my loving Father." I close my journal, but now what? At least I know what's been wrong with me, and probably with Nickers. I lost my first love. Now I need to find out how to get it back.

To be continued . . .

Lassoing the Truth

Winnie began centering her thoughts and goals on winning at the horse show, and she ended up miserable, not enjoying anything. God showed her that she'd lost her joyful first love for him. Like Winnie, we can get distracted, too busy with school, sports, and friends. Then we may neglect the most important relationship we'll ever have.

Whoa!

Journal about your day-to-day relationship with Jesus. Are you experiencing Christ's love and joy? Or have you been feeling too far away from God? If you don't feel close to Christ, ask the Lord to show you what keeps you from loving him first.

Dear God, please point out to me whenever I stop putting you first . . . and help me find the way back.

Giddyup!

On a yellow card, copy today's verse.

> I have this against you, that you have left your first love.
> Revelation 2:4, NASB
>
> Turn card over.

Give yourself a checkup:

1. List five things you thought about today. Now, number them in order, most to least, according to the amount of time you spent thinking about them.
2. List "Joy Moments" you had today, things you did or thought about that gave you joy. Number them in order according to how much joy each "Moment" brought you.

14

First Things

Remember from where you have fallen, and repent,
and do the deeds you did at first.

Revelation 2:5, NASB

Right away in the morning, I want to see Nickers. But first, I remember my Treasure Box. I find yesterday's card about losing my first love and reread it. This time, in the light, I see words at the bottom: "Turn card over." On the back of the card is the next verse in Revelation:

Remember from where you have fallen, and repent,
and do the deeds you did at first.
Revelation 2:5, NASB

Dear God,

You did it again! Yesterday you showed me that I left my first love, but I didn't know how to get it back. Now I get it: remember my first love and do the things I did at first. Plus, repent, which I really do.

When Mom gave me the Treasure Box, I wanted to read the verses all at once. But now I've gone days without reading any. In the beginning, I looked for you everywhere and saw you in people and nature. I paid attention in church because I wanted to learn more about you.

Please help me. You are so much busier than I am, yet you're always here for me to talk to. Thanks for waiting for me to show up.

I really love you! Winnie

I put on my best tan jeans and Mom's old black riding jacket and tall boots, then run to catch Dad before he and Madeline leave to hear some famous inventor in Akron.

"Don't you look spiffy!" Dad says, eyeing Mom's jacket like he recognizes it. "Good luck, Winnie. Hope you win the horse show. Sorry I can't be there."

I give him a hug.

In minutes I'm racing to the pasture. "Nickers!" *Lord, thanks for creating Nickers for me.* She keeps grazing, and I can't blame her. When I first got Nickers, I greeted her before dawn, blowing gently into her nostrils in the

Native American way. When she returned the favor, thanksgiving rose in my chest.

Nickers and I need to recapture *our* first love. I blow into her nostrils, and she finally returns the greeting. "I love you, Nickers."

Note to God: *I love YOU too!*

After grooming Nickers until she shines, I get out the jump saddle. I lift it to her back, but I can't do it. Even though I paid to enter the jumping event, even though Summer will call me a quitter, I lower the saddle. I love Nickers more. "Nickers, we're going to do the things we did at first."

I settle for a bitless hackamore, a no-bit bridle, and swing up bareback, figuring we've got time before picking up Catman. Like we've done so often, Nickers and I take a joy ride, where, eyes closed, I let her walk wherever she wants.

When I open my eyes, we're halfway to Coolidge Castle. Nickers stops beside three lawn ornaments that look like the Three Stooges. A fourth gnome could be Mrs. Coolidge shaking her finger at them.

Catman comes out, and Nickers and I move next to a stump. "Hop aboard!"

"Neat-O!" He slips on behind me, and we take the long way to the horse show grounds. At Mackall Pond, we spot M.

"Room for three?" he jokes. He checks his wrist as if he wore a watch. "Horse show?"

"Guess we lost track of time," I tell him. "It's okay.

Jumping class is first, and we're bowing out of that one. See you there, M!" We trot all the way, with Catman bouncing and laughing. When we're almost there, a squeaky microphone announces, "The judges have their decision in the jumping class."

Catman slides off. M joins him, and I ride to the arena in time to see Summer take her trophy. I've never seen this horse and wonder if she borrowed the Hanoverian or bought a new one. Hawk wins a yellow ribbon for third place. I catch her looking over at her not-applauding mother in the bleachers.

As Summer exits, she frowns over at me. "I knew you wouldn't really ride Wild Thing in the jumping competition."

I ignore her and shout congratulations to Hawk. "Towaco is amazing, and so are you!" Hawk smiles at me, but there's no happy behind it.

The microphone squeaks again. Summer's horse jolts, nearly throwing her. "Jumpers, please clear the arena. The next competition is the Pleasure Class."

"Let me out!" Summer shouts, exchanging the jumper for a fantastic black Morgan led to her by a Spidell's stable hand. "Winnie, you're in the way!"

"Nope. Nickers and I are in line for the Pleasure Class." Note to self: *Why not? We're both enjoying ourselves.*

Catman and M call out, "Cool!" "Right on!" and "Groovy!"

Nickers and I enter the arena with the other horses, though I'm the only one bareback. The ring is crowded as the announcer directs us to walk, trot, canter, then reverse. Every time I pass M and Catman, they cheer. Lizzy is sitting on Catman's shoulders. I guarantee nobody is enjoying this more than I am, except maybe Nickers.

Finally, the judge calls us to line up in the center. I end up next to Summer, who looks straight ahead as the judge walks around us, taking notes. "Judge?" Summer motions at me. "Her horse doesn't even have a saddle. You shouldn't have let them in."

The judge looks at me, and I smile at her. She's wearing a top hat and tuxedo. "It's a first for me," she admits, "but there's no rule against it."

Summer huffs as loud as a horse snorts. "Well, there should be a rule against it!" She says it so loud the mike picks it up.

Summer wins a fifth-place ribbon and almost refuses it, grabbing it at the last minute.

Nickers and I don't win, but I'm surprised how little I care. If they gave a prize for the horse and rider who got the most pleasure out of the *Pleasure* Class, we'd go home with a trophy. Nickers and I have recaptured our first love. And I've rediscovered my first love for Jesus. Something tells me that makes me a winner.

Lassoing the Truth

Winnie recaptured her first love for Jesus by doing the things she used to do and sharing each moment with her Lord. Her priorities shifted, and she felt the joy and love return to her relationship with God. It's easy to let something else take over first place in your life—a crush, an activity, a dream. If you believe you've lost your first love for Christ, God left instructions on how to regain that love: do the things you did when you first came to Christ.

Whoa!

When have you felt closest to God? What did that feel like? Journal about what you might do to fall in love with Jesus—again, or for the first time.

Dear Jesus, thank you for wanting a close, loving relationship with me. Remind me of the joy that comes with "first love," and help me do the things we did at first.

Giddyup!

Grab a yellow card and write today's verse on it:

Remember from where you have fallen, and repent, and do the deeds you did at first.
Revelation 2:5, NASB

Here's another verse you can copy for your Treasure Box.

You must love the LORD your God with all your heart, all your soul, and all your strength.
Deuteronomy 6:5

Today, do one thing that used to make you feel close to God.

15

Reading Horses

He knows the secrets of every heart.

Psalm 44:21

Although I love my new client's horse, I'm not looking forward to another visit from the owner.

I pull out my Treasure Verse and go for a purple, anxious card.

He knows the secrets of every heart.
Psalm 44:21

Dear God,

I've been trying to see how this could help me with Sophia, my new client's daughter. You know I can read horses and understand their clues and signals, their secrets. But people? Not so much. For example, Sophia owns this mare, Valentine, a beautiful red-chestnut American Saddle Horse. I think Valentine is coming along nicely. She even likes our time together, most of the time. Yesterday, the mare answered my cues and commands in the round pen. Then I rode her for an hour. She loved it.

I know that because I can read horses. Ears back, angry. Ears forward, curious. Ears up and back, curious, paying attention, listening, and doing all right. Tail stiff, scared—well, I'll stop. You made horses with ways to communicate if we pay attention.

On the other hand, so far, I can't figure out Sophia at all. And her mother says I'm supposed to make sure she can ride Valentine safely. To be honest—which you always want me to be—Valentine and I are a little afraid of angry Sophia.

Lord, you know the secrets of every heart. It sure would be a big help if you could whisper a few of Sophia's secrets to me. She doesn't seem to like her horse. Or me. But thanks for helping me understand Valentine. Please help me understand Sophia too.

Love, Winnie

Things are going great as I ride Valentine through the pasture before moving to the round pen. I have to keep her saddled for Sophia's sake, but I long to throw off the saddle and have a better feel for when the mare's back tightens. I watch her ears, now straight up at attention. When we canter, she flicks one ear back and the other ear forward.

Sophia should have been here an hour ago, so I ride into the round pen. Valentine responds to my voice cues: "Walk!" "Trot!" "Canter." I work on her left lead because she seems to favor the right-leg lead circling in either direction. Sophia still hasn't shown up.

It's getting late, and I promised Nickers a ride. My sweet horse grazes near the round pen and lifts her head to watch me ride Valentine. She must be wondering why I'm not riding *her.*

Finally giving up on Sophia, I unsaddle Valentine, cool her off, groom her again, then turn her out. I'm getting Nickers ready for a long ride when Sophia strolls into the barn. She's dressed for a tea party, cashmere pink pants and matching sweater that looks soft as a foal's fuzz.

Note to self: *Not my job to tell people how not to dress for a horse ride.*

Sophia yawns. "Where's my horse? You're supposed to train *my* horse, not *your* horse." If Sophia were a horse, she'd be the last truly wild breed, a Przewalski from Mongolia. Those ancient horses often have trouble bonding with others in the herd. Sophia actually stamps her foot, which I thought only bratty kids did on junk TV.

She looks ready to bite me. "I'll leave right now if you aren't going to tell me what you've done with my horse!"

Note to self: *Hmmm . . . To tell, or not to tell?*

I realize I'm still holding Nickers's hoof and the hoof pick. I let her foot down. "Valentine is in the pasture. You're so late I didn't think you were coming."

Ignoring the comment, Sophia barges through Nickers's stall and out to the pasture. "Valentine, come here!" she yells. When Valentine doesn't accept the invitation, Sophia shouts louder, "I mean it! Get over here right now!"

I ease past her. "I'll get her."

"No you won't!" Sophia nearly screams. "She's *my* horse. *I'll* get her." She grabs the leadrope out of my hand and storms toward Valentine. Worry wrinkles form at the mare's eyes, and she tucks in her tail. When Sophia gets close, Valentine's ears go flat back. Her lips curl, and she snorts.

"Sophia, stop! Valentine's scared!"

"She *should* be scared!" Sophia yells as she reaches for the halter.

I see the white of Valentine's eyes, the fear taking over. I run up behind Sophia and reach Valentine's halter before Sophia can. "Back off, Sophia! She's going to bite you!"

I take the leadrope from her and snap it onto the halter, fully expecting Sophia to attack both of us. "Easy, girl," I tell Valentine, rubbing the whorl in her white blaze. I scratch her jowl until her back stops twitching and her head quits tossing like M listening to crazy music.

When I move to face Sophia and whatever abuse she'll hurl, she's turned her back on me. "I know you're mad, Sophia. But I was afraid Valentine would bite you."

Instead of yelling at me, she runs to the barn. When she glances over her shoulder, I see that she's crying.

To be continued . . .

Lassoing the Truth

Winnie is great at reading a horse's emotions. She observes gestures, expressions, and body language. Those clues give her a window into what horses are feeling. Humans, on the other hand, can be a mystery. Like Winnie, most of us need to pay closer attention to what might be bothering a friend or family member. After praying, the first step in helping people is to try to understand them. God knows their secrets, so he can help you.

Whoa!

Can you tell when an animal feels scared or sick or happy or angry? Journal in detail about your observations and how they hint at an animal's feelings. Now, write about the cues you believe you give off when you're scared, sick, happy, or angry.

Dear God, please help me pay attention and learn from observing animals and people.

Giddyup!

Write today's verse onto a purple, anxious card.

He knows the secrets of every heart.
Psalm 44:21

If you have a secret deep in your heart, you can talk about it to God, who loves you at all times.

16

Reading People

He has showered his kindness on us,
along with all wisdom and understanding.

Ephesians 1:8

I watch my teen client, Sophia, walk away from me, away from her horse, up the drive, and out of sight.

"Winnie, why was Sophia upset?" If my little sis, Lizzy, were a horse, she'd be a faithful Trakehner, a light, warm-blooded breed, great for dressage and friendship.

"I wish I knew. One minute I thought she was going to bite my head off, and the next, she ran away . . . crying. I didn't think she cared that much about Valentine."

Lizzy prays, "Take care of Sophia, Lord. Help Winnie to help her." She turns to me. "Too bad you don't understand her signals like you do her horse's."

The bright sun disappears as puffy clouds turn the blue sky to gray. Nickers whinnies from the pasture, then prances back to the barn. Valentine follows. Horses are great forecasters. "We better go in, Lizzy. I smell a storm."

In minutes, thunder rumbles. Then rain dances on willows and shagbark hickories. We make it in just as sheets of rain pound the roof and shake the windows. Dad's in the basement working on a battery-operated coffee maker-mug. Lizzy's phone rings, probably her friend Geri, who hates storms.

I go to my room and thumb through my Treasure Box. I stop when I see my name, written in Mom's no-nonsense handwriting.

Winnie, he has showered his kindness on us,
along with all wisdom and understanding.
Ephesians 1:8

I pull out my journal and begin.

Dear God,

It's not easy to be kind to Sophia. I can't understand her. But this verse says you showered me with kindness and gave me wisdom and understanding. That sounds like a promise, so it must be true, even though I don't feel wise or understanding, or like showing kindness to Sophia. Please help me "read" Sophia like I do her horse.

Love, Winnie

In the morning, I find Nickers and Valentine both caked in mud. I curry Nickers, then put Valentine in the cross ties to groom. I watch for Sophia, but I doubt she'll show.

I've barely started on Valentine when Sophia slinks in wearing jeans, a silky shirt, and a ponytail. Her eyes are red-rimmed.

"Hey, Sophia."

She nods but twists her lips. Horses do that when they're scared, ready to bolt.

"I could use some help. Valentine played in the mud with Nickers."

Not waiting for an answer, I grab a firm brush for myself and toss her the currycomb I was using.

She catches it and eventually moves it over Valentine's neck. After a few strokes, she says, "The mud's not coming off." She stamps her foot, like Nickers does when she gets frustrated.

"You're doing it right, Sophia. She likes your soft hand. If you brushed hard enough for mud to come off with only a couple of strokes, it could hurt her."

We groom in silence, but I see the way Sophia bites her bottom lip, like Lizzy when she concentrates.

"I'll get the saddle." I point out Valentine's saddle blanket. "Better double-check that. Valentine won't like it if she's got a burr under the blanket."

Sophia shakes the blanket and mutters, "I know people like that."

The way she says it, I know she's not joking. "Me too. My dad gets cranky when he can't get his inventions to work. Or when he can't get an odd job and needs the money."

"Not my dad," Sophia says. "When he gets upset, he buys me stuff, like this horse."

I was trying to make her feel better. Now I want to defend my dad, but something stops me. Sophia swallows hard and pretends to study her shiny leather boots. I don't know what to say, so I ask God to keep me from saying the wrong thing. "Sophia, why does your dad buy you things when he's upset?"

No answer.

Note to self: *When in doubt, keep your mouth shut. So much for reading people.*

I go to get the saddle, and when I return, Sophia says, "Dad gets upset at my mom. He yells. She takes off. He buys me a horse. Mom stays away."

"That's hard. My mom's gone too. In heaven." I try to imagine how it would feel to have your mom be away on purpose.

"They're getting a divorce, and I'm old enough to choose which one I want to live with. Dad becomes Disneyland Dad, the fun one. I don't even know if either of them wants me. They act like they do, but I think they just want to get back at each other."

Before I can think of something to say, Sophia says, "Can we take Valentine out?"

Valentine is great when we saddle her. I let Sophia lead her to the pasture. "She's liking this, isn't she?" Sophia's face shines with a joy she's kept a secret.

"She is!" I show her how to scratch Valentine's chest, making her horse sway with delight. "Scratch harder on the hindquarters." Valentine nearly dances from pleasure. It doesn't take much people-sense to read that Sophia is delighting in her horse too.

We end the session and agree to get Sophia in the saddle tomorrow. Before she leaves the barn, Sophia hugs Valentine.

"Looks to me like you've gained a friend," I observe.

"Or two," she calls over her shoulder as she walks away.

Lassoing the Truth

Winnie wasn't great at reading people's emotions until she started paying attention to Sophia and discovering people cues (biting or twisting lips, rolling eyes, folding arms, tapping or stomping feet, etc.). Understanding a friend—or an enemy—requires paying attention. If you want to help someone, you can always ask God for wisdom in figuring out how to show them God's kindness.

Whoa!

Prayerfully pay attention to someone in your family, or at school, who's been acting angrier or sadder or more distant than usual. Journal your observations to God and ask for wisdom and understanding. Ask the Lord to help you help others.

Dear God, please help me be more sensitive to people around me who are hurting.

Giddyup!

Write today's verse onto a yellow, confused card. Add your name at the beginning.

____________, he has showered his kindness on us,
along with all wisdom and understanding.
Ephesians 1:8

Find a couple of other cards from your Treasure Box, verses that you'd like to personalize. Write in your name, because God is talking to you.

17

Whisper His Name

Pray like this: Our Father in heaven,
may your name be kept holy.

Matthew 6:9

I don't like how I feel this morning. I have a bad-day-at-school taste in my mouth, but I don't know why. I sure don't want to feel this way all day, so I reach for my Treasure Box and pull a green card because I want a happy day. Right away I recognize the Lord's Prayer:

Pray like this: Our Father in heaven,
may your name be kept holy.
Matthew 6:9

Dear God,

Thank you! Now I remember where that bad taste came from. All day yesterday I felt bombarded by kids using "God" and "Jesus" like swear words. I counted eight saying, "Oh, God!" (not at the same time). Pretty sure they meant it like "Oh, man!" or "Yikes! I didn't see that coming!"

I lost track of how many times I heard "Jesus!" in the hall. Like two girls were laughing, and one said, "Jesus, you've got to be kidding!"

It hurt my heart each time. I'm sorry (even though I'm not the one who "took your name in vain," as Pastor Ralph says).

Sometimes I'd like to smack kids who use your name like an exclamation point.

Sorry about that.

Love, Winnie

The roads are too muddy for me to ride the back bike, so Lizzy and I sit together in the back of the bus. I stare out the window at a sky trying to keep the sun away. But the sun is starting to poke through, making the wet street shine. A few clouds look soft enough to float on. God created so much beauty for us, and there's not much appreciation for it at school.

I turn to Lizzy. "What do you do when someone says 'Jesus' or 'God' like swear words? It's really starting to bother me."

She breaks into a smile—not the reaction I'd expected. "That's great, Winnie! It says a lot that it bothers you. Hearing Jesus' name used like that hurts me. I figure if it hurts me, it's probably hurting God. So I whisper 'Jesus' or 'God' with all the love I have. Or I'll whisper, 'I love your name!' It helps me, and I hope it helps Jesus, because I'll bet hearing his name used like swearing makes him sad."

It doesn't take long to test Lizzy's theory. Before I'm even inside the school building, I see a sixth grader drop his unzipped backpack, spilling papers and junk. He mutters, "Jesus!" By the lockers three laughing classmates are huddled over a cell phone, and one screams, "Oh, God!"

My stomach feels like a colt is kicking its way out. *I'm sorry, God. I love your name and the name of Jesus.* Lizzy was right about it making me feel better.

But it doesn't change things the rest of the morning. I hear those same thoughtless exclamations over and over.

Friday lunch is the best part of the school week. High school students can join middle schoolers for lunch if they sign up. Catman and M signed up for the whole year. By the time I make it to our table, they've saved me a seat between them. Barker sits across from us, next to Grady and Peyton, an eighth-grade couple.

Grady stabs a breaded mushroom. "God, what is this stuff?"

I glance at Catman, knowing he understands how I feel about this. I start to tell him that I'm whispering to God and it helps when Eric, the kid next to Catman, slams down his fork and says, "Jesus, this food stinks!"

I'm in the middle of telling Jesus I love his name when

Catman jumps to his feet, looks frantically down the lunch table, then all around the cafeteria. "Where?" he shouts, like a fan when a celebrity is sighted. Nobody answers. He looks expectantly at Grady, then Eric, and asks, "Dudes, where is he?"

The clatter of silverware, the laughter, and all talking disappear, leaving an eerie silence never before heard in this lunchroom. Finally, Eric asks, "Where's who?"

"Jesus," Catman says.

"You're crazy, Catman," Grady says, glancing to Eric.

"I'm not the one blaming Jesus for the food, shouting out his name, but claiming he's not really here." Catman sits down again, but nobody looks away. "Truth is, Jesus *is* here, and God is everywhere. Even if you didn't really see him, you can always call out to him for real. But pay attention, man! The Good News is that he loves you and will answer your call."

From the table behind us comes applause—from Lizzy and everyone at her table. Barker stands up and hoots. M holds up a piece of bread nibbled into the shape of a cross.

Barker, all smiles, hands me his napkin before I realize I'm crying. I think I've just witnessed the best thing that ever happened in our school.

That night I lie in bed repeating the Lord's Prayer Mom had us memorize: *Our Father who art in heaven, hallowed be thy name.* Pastor Ralph said *hallowed* means *holy*. I close my eyes, and my mind camera has recorded Catman at high noon. I fall asleep watching him keep God's name holy in the lunchroom of Ashland, Ohio.

Lassoing the Truth

Winnie loved God so much that she grew upset at the misuse of the name of Jesus and God. She and Catman wanted to keep God's name holy. In the same way, we can't let ourselves get so used to the misuse of God's holy name or the name of Jesus that it doesn't bother us. It's probably not best to handle situations the way Catman did in the story, but we can make sure that *we* always honor the names of Jesus and God.

Whoa!

Jesus Christ is Immanuel, God with Us; Savior; Wonderful Counselor; Prince of Peace; the Alpha and Omega (First and Last); the Almighty One; Son of God; the Word; the Way, the Truth, and the Life; the Light of the World; I Am; and many other glorious names. Journal about what Jesus' name means to you.

Lord, would you help me whisper your name throughout the day to let you know how much I love you and your name?

Giddyup!

On a joyful green card, write today's verse:

Pray like this: Our Father in heaven,
may your name be kept holy.
Matthew 6:9

Then go to your Bible and read the full Lord's Prayer in Matthew 6:7-13.

18

Honesty

You desire honesty from the womb,
teaching me wisdom even there.

Psalm 51:6

I am amazed at the sunshine and blue skies that burst through the window when I shove back my horse curtains because inside of me, storms are brewing under a dark, concrete sky.

I skip breakfast and go straight to the barn. The sunshine lied to me, so I didn't wear my warm jacket, and now I'm cold. I exercise Towaco, Valentine, and Buddy, not even trying to figure out why I feel yucky, angry, and sad. Even when I take a short ride on Nickers, I tell myself I'm fine, nothing's wrong. But I guess the sky isn't the only liar.

Lunch is over, but Lizzy's left a peanut-butter-and-honey sandwich for me. I take it to my room and get a yellow card from my Treasure Box, though I could have picked any color except green.

You desire honesty from the womb,
teaching me wisdom even there.
Psalm 51:6

Dear God,

I don't want to write to you about this. (And yes, I know you know my thoughts before I know them.) But you say you want honesty from me, right? Well, here goes. I miss Mom. Yesterday when I wore her green sweater, I think I smelled her hair and maybe horse. When we used to ride double on Chief, our big ol' plow horse, we'd gallop, and Mom's hair would fly into my face. She taught me everything I know about horse gentling, but she would have taught me so much more if . . .

The ache of missing Mom feels like getting kicked by a bronco, and it makes me mad. Then deep down inside, I blame you. I'm sorry, but you asked for honesty. You could have kept Mom from going out in a blizzard, no matter how hard I begged her to go and get my birthday horse. You could have kept her tires from skidding, held the pickup and trailer to the road, given her *vision through the mass of snowflakes, moved the telephone pole. You can do anything, God. You could have saved her. Or waited until she turned a hundred years old. But you took her from me.*

I'm sorry. I didn't know I was going to write all this. I didn't even let myself form those thoughts because I'm supposed to worship you and not doubt anything. I need to go. I'm sorry I've splotched this letter with tears. I'm sorry about everything, including that I can't write in this journal any longer.

I run to the bathroom and splash cold water on my face. When I come out, Lizzy is waiting for me. "Is it Mom, Winnie?" She puts her arms around me, and I burst into tears. She holds me until I stop crying and pull away, only to see her crying now.

"Lizzy, I know you miss Mom too, but do you ever regret moving away from the Willis Wyoming Ranch?" We sit on the top stair together.

Lizzy grins. "I loved Wyoming because of all the lizards and desert bugs and reptiles. How can you not love a state with a horned toad as the state reptile, even though the 'horned toad' is actually a lizard?" Her grin dissolves, and her eyes tear up again. "But God's ways are higher than our ways. There are lots of things, like Mom, we'll never understand until we're face-to-face with Jesus and become more like him. Until then, it just makes sense to trust him."

Lizzy leaves to start dinner, but I stay sitting and thinking about Mom. Only this time I close my eyes and sense that I'm not alone. Jesus is holding my hand, his other arm wrapped around me. He knows why Mom had to join him early, even if I still don't. But I bet I'll understand when I join Mom and Jesus. And until then, he won't let go of my hand.

I sit by my bedroom window and write where I left off. It feels like days ago instead of hours.

Dear God—I'm back.

I wanted to thank you for inviting me to be honest with you. Just opening up my heart and letting my rotten thoughts out helped me realize how much you love me. Thanks for forgiving me for blaming you. How could I even think you didn't care? You died for me! And Mom. When my mind shoots me a picture of the accident and Mom's head on the steering wheel, I'll remember Mom's favorite picture of Jesus on the cross, going through what he did to pay for every wrong thought and action I have. Then I'll recall her other favorite picture, the one of the Resurrection.

Thank you for the gift of my mom, loaded with so much love and kindness and horse smarts that I should be set for the rest of my life on earth. Thanks for keeping Mom safe in heaven, where we'll all be together forever . . . with you.

Love, Winnie the Horse Gentler, like my mom.
Honestly.

PS Plus, I love that you promise to wipe away every tear.

Lassoing the Truth

Winnie didn't want to be honest with God because she didn't want to be honest with herself and her feelings. When she opened herself to God, journaling even her worst thoughts and emotions, God's comfort could reach her. Are you ever tied up in knots, so upset and angry that you don't want to try to figure out why? Talking or writing honestly to God can be a great first step toward untangling your thoughts and emotions.

Whoa!

Are there any conflicting thoughts or feelings you don't really want to admit to yourself? Any confusion? Journal honestly to God. God knows your thoughts before you do. And nothing you can tell God could make him love you less.

____

____

____

____

____

____

____

Dear God, thank you for loving me even when I'm ungrateful and angry or frustrated. Help me be honest with you always.

Giddyup!

Make a card for today's Treasure Verse. Choose the color that best describes how you're feeling right now, and remember to be honest with God as you tell him about that emotion.

You desire honesty from the womb,
teaching me wisdom even there.
Psalm 51:6

Try journaling again, choosing another secret you want to honestly talk about with God.

19

The Great Burden Trade

Jesus said, "Come to me, all of you who are weary and carry heavy burdens, and I will give you rest."

Matthew 11:28

I feel like a worn-out mare with twin foals. I have two reports to write, a science test to study for, and math homework that might as well be in hieroglyphics. Plus, the Mustang Rescue dropped off two yearlings since Mustang Sam is doing so well.

Dad's "friend" Madeline is over *again*. She's brought her son, Mason, and I'm trying to get Mason and Buddy, his little filly, to be friends again.

I love Mason and Buddy. Mason is kind of a miracle, although most people just see the different part of him. He makes me feel something deep inside, like God did something special creating Mason and talks to him all the time. Mason can disappear right before your eyes and stare into space, blocking out the world. That's something I wish I could do sometimes. Buddy was an orphan foal born in our barn. Mason loved Buddy from day one, so I gave them to each other. Mason named *her* "Buddy."

All was well until two weeks ago Buddy and Mason sneezed at the same time, sending both into hiding, which was pretty funny at the time. But not so funny now that they're terrified of each other.

I want to get Mason to the barn, but he's sitting in a pile of leaves in what I call his block-out moment, when he stares at whatever he sees that we don't. As I sit beside him, Catman comes up and sits next to us. I study Mason's round face with one dimple on his right cheek, his thin, wispy white-blond hair, and blue eyes wide behind thick lenses.

Madeline, Mason's overprotective mother, comes out, snatches up her son, and returns to our house. So much for getting Mason and Buddy to be friends again. "What I wouldn't give to block out the world," I mutter.

"Deep," Catman says.

I start complaining to Catman how everything is piling up on me when we hear a squeal followed by a *thud*. We race to the barn to find the new Mustangs fighting. At the sight of me, they join forces and race out to the pasture.

I feed Nickers and wish I could ride my horse away from it all. "I haven't ridden Nickers for a week! I told the rescue I could get the Mustangs gentled before the auction, and there's Buddy, and the new boarder, plus Towaco to exercise."

"Heavy." Catman fills the troughs with hay. "Sorry. I've got to split. Gnome duty."

Alone again, I feel the weight of all I have to do. Nickers nudges me, and I bury my face in her mane. "You need a ride as much as I do, don't you, girl?"

Instead, I work with Buddy without Mason, then muck stalls.

Lizzy has a grilled peanut-butter-and-cheese sandwich waiting for me. "I'll be leaving soon for Geri's sleepover. Don't forget you have to get Dad's dinner tonight."

Of course, I forgot. Note to self: *Wonder if Dad likes bread. And pickles?*

Lizzy wipes the table with a dish towel. "So what was your Treasure Verse today?"

"I didn't read one." I take a big bite of my sandwich and run upstairs. Definitely a purple-card day.

Jesus said, "Come to me, all of you who are weary and carry heavy burdens, and I will give you rest."
Matthew 11:28

Rest? Note to self: *I can't remember the last time I got to rest.*

"Lizzy!" I take the card and race to the kitchen, where Lizzy is wiping counters. "Sit! Please!" I scoot two chairs together.

"Are you okay, Winnie?" She sits and takes the card I'm shoving in her face.

"I need to know what this means, Lizzy. I've been weary and carrying heavy burdens, but what about rest?"

Lizzy leans over and gives me a one-armed hug. "Isn't it wonderful that Jesus himself is giving you the answer? Okay. You know how our Amish neighbors yoke their horses together to pull a wagon?" I nod. "The load would be too heavy for one horse. You've been trying to do everything yourself. Jesus wants to share *his* load so you can rest."

I'm taking it in, picturing myself trying to pull a wagon-load of lumber by myself. And Jesus is shaking his head, saying, "Come on. I'll share my lighter burden of flowers with you so you can find rest."

I grab Lizzy for a two-armed hug. "Thanks, Lizzy!"

I start for the barn, then go back for my journal, climb to the hayloft, and write.

Dear God,

I'm sorry I haven't journaled to you lately. I thought I didn't have the time. I was wrong. If I'd listened to you earlier, I might not have wasted time trying to do everything on my own.

I think I'm already feeling lighter, like not everything depends on me. Please help me remember you and I are sharing your load. I give you mine, and ask for your rest.

Love, Winnie

As soon as I come down from the loft and see Buddy and the Mustangs, and the boarders, the heavy burden comes back. I feel like I need to work all the horses right now. Then I remember—I am not alone.

I don't exactly win over the Mustangs, though they do let me groom them. Every few minutes, I whisper to Jesus, thanking him for teaming up with me.

I have a good ride on Towaco and a glorious gallop with Nickers, where peace splashes over me like a spring thaw.

At the end of the day, I don't get everything done that I thought I *had to*, but Jesus brought rest, and we'll share the load tomorrow . . . and forever.

Lassoing the Truth

Winnie felt weighed down with everything she had to do. But when she understood that Jesus wanted her to join him and share his lighter load, she found rest and joy in him. If you ever feel overwhelmed with all you have to do, you can ask Jesus for help. Being aware of Christ's presence and knowing Jesus offers help and peace can give you rest from the pressures you put on yourself.

Whoa!

What are the things you feel pressured to do? Do you have any "burdens"? Journal to God about each one. Then write what it will mean for you to share in *his* plans for tomorrow.

____

____

____

____

____

____

____

Dear God, I'm sorry I've been acting like the world depends on me, instead of you. Please help me to find rest in you.

Giddyup!

Write today's verse on a purple card.

Jesus said, "Come to me, all of you who are weary and carry heavy burdens, and I will give you rest."
Matthew 11:28

Pray that God will help you share this verse with someone struggling with a heavy burden. Ask God to show you how you can help. Then check out the rest of Jesus' invitation in your Bible:

Take my yoke upon you. Let me teach you, because I am humble and gentle at heart, and you will find rest for your souls. For my yoke is easy to bear, and the burden I give you is light.
Matthew 11:29-30

20

Rewards

Watch out! Don't do your good deeds publicly, to be admired by others, for you will lose the reward from your Father in heaven.

Matthew 6:1

Dear God,

I'm saving my Treasure Verse for tonight, but I wanted to write a thank-you to you for sending me Mario, the black-as-midnight Andalusian. The Hathaways, who are richer than the Spidells, brought their horse to me! And all I have to do is get him over his sudden fear of everything. Plus, they're paying me twice what most clients pay, even though I told them my regular fee. I even get a bonus if I can "restore Mario" in a week for a Cleveland show.

Yikes! Gotta bounce, as M would say. I want to visit Mario before I leave for school.

Love, Winnie

When Mario comes into the barn for breakfast, I try to join him in the stall, but he grabs a mouthful of oats and races to the pasture, nearly crushing me against the feed trough.

Back-biking to school, I tell Catman all about Mario and how I'm going to gentle him. "I wasn't their first choice," I admit. "Mrs. Hathaway told me Mario was at Spidell's Stable-Mart while they were on vacation in Paris—France, not Paris, Ohio. When they returned, Mario was scared of everything. They were so angry at Spidell's, they asked around for the name of someone who could help their horse. One of the Spidell's stable workers mentioned me. Okay—it was Dad, Spidell's odd-job man."

"Deep," he says, taking his hands from the handlebars. He steers with his legs, kind of like riding with no bridle.

"Can't you see the look on Mrs. Hathaway's face when I hand over her calm horse in time for the Cleveland Horse Show?"

The first person I see in homeroom is Summer Spidell, surrounded by her herd of girls. "Winnie?" She curves her index finger at me. "We were just talking about you."

Note to self: *This can't be good.*

"Daddy said you got stuck with that crazy horse he sent away. I guess you need every horse you can get."

"Are we talking about the same horse? Mario the Andalusian?"

"We didn't keep him long enough to know his name," she says. "We were glad to get rid of him."

My insides buck. "That's not the way I heard it." She

gives me her Are-you-crazy-as-well-as-stupid? look, which makes me add, "No, I'm the horse gentler the Hathaways chose to work with their champion."

Sal slides off the teacher's desk. "*The* Hathaways?"

I nod, smiling inside and out.

After school I talk Catman and M into coming over to help with Mario. After four tries to catch the horse, I'm forced to trap Mario in the barn.

Once I get him into the cross ties, M and I start brushing. But Mario won't let M near him. "M, could you help Catman string the plastic flags between the two hickories? We need to get Mario used to movement and noise."

The gelding's muscles tense when I brush him. I should keep brushing until he's relaxed, but it's taking forever. So finally, I saddle him with a lightweight English saddle. He sidesteps as much as he can in cross ties, but he doesn't throw a fit. Good enough. I expect a fuss when I slip on the Weymouth bridle the owners left for me, a double bridle used in upper dressage levels. It has two bits and two sets of reins. But Mario seems fine with it.

When I mount the seventeen-hand gelding, he startles, and I nearly miss the stirrup. But once we're in the pasture, he rides nice. M gives me a thumbs-up, and Catman says, "Choice! Righteous."

I'm wondering if I could trot by the flags. But just as we're a horse's length from them, Mario stops. I squeeze my knees and click my tongue. Nothing. I try turning him to get him started. No way. Everything I try fails.

"What if you lead him?" Catman asks. M nods like a woodpecker pecks.

Sighing, I dismount and lead Mario to the flags, but he has to smell each one before he'll advance. I don't have time for this.

I get back in the saddle, intending to ride the flag line. Suddenly, a strong wind makes the flags crackle. Mario rears so high I'm afraid he'll go over backwards. Catman and M, arms out, shuffle around the horse, ready to catch me.

"I'm okay." But Mario isn't. I can't ride him close to the line. Or the fence. Or the barrels. Or trees.

M, Catman, and I don't say much in the barn while I cool Mario down. I thank them for helping me waste the day with this horse.

As they're leaving, so does the sun, disappearing beneath a tiny glow at the horizon. Catman turns back. "Winnie, chill. Rushing's a downer."

"A bummer," M adds.

Note to self: *They're right. Why did I have to rush the poor horse?*

Later, I flip through my Treasure Box cards and choose the first blue card where Mom wrote in my name.

Watch out, Winnie! Don't do your good deeds publicly, to be admired by others, for you will lose the reward from your Father in heaven.

Matthew 6:1

To be continued . . .

Lassoing the Truth

Winnie wanted to show up Summer by training Mario fast. And she wanted the admiration of the Hathaways, so much so that she forgot to focus on Mario—or God. Everyone likes to be admired. But if that's our goal, we end up losing our reward from our Father in heaven. If you're focused on an earthly reward now, like Winnie was, you can change your focus to God.

Whoa!

Have you ever tried too hard to be admired by people? Journal about it and ask God to show you areas in your life where you may be too worried about what people think.

____

____

____

____

____

____

____

____

Dear God, please show me when I forget that my goal should be to seek you, not admiration on earth.

Giddyup!

Copy the Treasure Verse from today onto a yellow card if you think this verse would be great to read when you feel confused. If you think the verse is one you'd like to find when you're sad, use a blue card. Write your own name in the blank.

Watch out, ___________! Don't do your good deeds publicly, to be admired by others, for you will lose the reward from your Father in heaven.

Matthew 6:1

21

Who's Your Audience?

Obviously, I'm not trying to win the approval of people, but of God. If pleasing people were my goal, I would not be Christ's servant.

Galatians 1:10

Dear God,

Thanks for last night's verse and having Mom write me into it. Matthew 6:1 stayed in the front of my brain and was there every time I woke up:

> Watch out, Winnie! Don't do your good deeds publicly, to be admired by others, for you will lose the reward from your Father in heaven.

You and Mom nailed it, as always. I've been trying to gentle Mario for all the wrong reasons—to show Summer what I could do and to impress the Hathaways and be rewarded. But I chose the wrong place for a reward. I'd rather get it in heaven.

And then this morning after quite a search, I found the church bulletin where I'd written a verse from Pastor Ralph's sermon last month. I thought it was the verse from yesterday, but it's another one about being a people pleaser:

Obviously, I'm not trying to win the approval of people,
but of God. If pleasing people were my goal,
I would not be Christ's servant.
Galatians 1:10

This verse is so perfect for helping me see where I went wrong with Mario. Instead of wanting Christ's approval, I was yearning for people's approval. Thanks for showing me, forgiving me, and loving me. I'm copying this verse on a yellow card.

Love, Winnie

I grain the horses, taking a little extra time with Mario, brushing him and singing. I love Saturday mornings. Catman and M said they'd help me with Mario this afternoon, but I have time to go on a much-needed ride. I pack a boiled egg, half a bologna sandwich, a giant pickle, and two apples, plus sugar cubes, and Nickers and I head for our favorite picnic spot for brunch. On our way to the woods, the *KNOCK-KNOCK-KNOCK* of a pileated woodpecker matches the beat of Nickers's hooves. Then songbirds give us a concert as we share our meal under the oak tree.

When I get back, Catman and M have set up plastic flags in the far corner of the pasture. Nickers and I charge the guys, and we all laugh when they scurry out of the way. I can sense Mario watching the fun from inside the barn. I hop off Nickers, race to the tack room, and bring out a big ball with a rubber grab handle. Fearful as ever, Mario rears, then gallops away. I whisper to God, thanking him that however this turns out, Christ approves of me.

Nickers knows what's coming. I toss her the ball and run the other way until I hear hooves thundering up behind me. I turn to see her racing at me, the ball handle between her teeth. She keeps running but drops the ball at my feet. "Catman! M! Come on!"

I don't have to ask twice. M grabs the ball and kicks it. He and Catman run after it. Catman gets there first and head-bangs the ball to Nickers. She rears, then muzzles it away. M dives for it. The four of us play for a long time while Mario edges closer. When I call him to join us, he takes a step back, looking ready to bolt. "Keep playing," I tell M and Catman, who really haven't stopped.

Humming, I head for the barn, sidetracking a bit to give Mario a good scratch as I pass. When I come out with a leadrope, Mario shows the whites of his eyes, as if I'm holding a snake. But I'm too fast for him and snap the lead to his halter. Catman rolls the ball in Mario's general direction. Mario stands his ground. Not sure I'd call this progress, but it's kind of fun.

"Catch!" M produces a bag of apples and tosses them to everybody, including the horses. Mario takes his time but finally downs one.

We pick up where we left off, and Mario gets used to the scary ball. A few times, he nudges the ball, though he doesn't pick it up.

I'm getting tired, but not frustrated, when Lizzy comes out and takes her seat on the fence post. "You guys want to join us for dinner?"

Dinner? I'm surprised to see the low sun blinking behind our woods, close to the horizon.

"What about working Mario?" M asks.

"We'll get there," I answer. "Mario has time."

Dad is at the table, dishing up bowls of macaroni and tuna. Lizzy sets down a glass vase of carrots and celery sticks. She makes us hold hands. Catman's fingers cover my whole hand as Lizzy thanks God for food and friends and lizards and . . . until Dad says, "Amen."

"What scared Mario when the Spidells stabled him?" Lizzy asks.

I put a big blob of Tuna-roni on my plate. "That's what I'd like to know."

Dad looks up, and a piece of 'roni is stuck to his chin. "Probably what scares me when I'm doing odd jobs at Stable-Mart—motorcycles. Loud motorcycles. Summer's brother, Robert, and his biker buddies drive like monkeys, laughing like hyenas, cycles roaring like angry lions through the stable. I hide in the tack room."

"That would do it, all right," I say.

M sets down his spoon. "Poor Mario."

Lizzy puts her hand on my arm. "Oh, Winnie, can you help Mario by tomorrow night when the Hathaways come to check?"

I shake my head. "Probably not by tomorrow. It's okay though. I loved taking time with Mario today." I'd planned to surprise everybody and have Mario ready to go. The Hathaways would have been pleased all right, and I would have loved that. But I don't serve the Hathaways or other people. I'm a servant of Christ.

M, totally done with dinner, walks his empty plate to the sink. "So, does that mean we can play with Mario again?"

Catman consults my face, jumps up from the table, and answers for me. "Affirmative! And groovy!"

I admit it hurts a little that I won't get that bonus from the Hathaways. But as we all walk to the barn under the Milky Way, with cricket music and the smell of horse surrounding us, I whisper thanks to God. I gaze at the stars and feel the comfort of knowing I'm serving God, and he's pleased.

Lassoing the Truth

When Winnie stopped trying to please people and instead focused on pleasing God, she began to enjoy her work. It's so easy to become a "people pleaser"—but what a joy when you become a God pleaser instead.

Whoa!

Are you worried about pleasing a certain person—someone special, or a "herd"? Journal about it to God and describe what you're doing to please people. What does it feel like to be admired by other people? Why do you think you want others to notice you and think well of you? Ask God to help you be Christ's servant and a God pleaser instead of a people pleaser.

Dear God, I'm sorry that I've wasted so much time trying to please people. You are the One I want to please and serve.

Giddyup!

The Bible says a lot about pleasing God, rather than people. Copy today's verse on a yellow card.

Obviously, I'm not trying to win the approval of people,
but of God. If pleasing people were my goal,
I would not be Christ's servant.
Galatians 1:10

Next, read the following verses and copy any additional verses you'd like onto cards of whatever color makes sense to you.

Fearing people is a dangerous trap,
but trusting the LORD means safety.
Proverbs 29:25

Finally, dear brothers and sisters, we urge you in the name of the Lord Jesus to live in a way that pleases God, as we have taught you. You live this way already, and we encourage you to do so even more.

1 Thessalonians 4:1

We speak as messengers approved by God to be entrusted with the Good News. Our purpose is to please God, not people. He alone examines the motives of our hearts.

1 Thessalonians 2:4

They loved human praise more than the praise of God.

John 12:43

22

Cheater

The Lord your God is going ahead of you.
He will fight for you, just as you saw him do in Egypt.

Deuteronomy 1:30

I am standing in front of the teacher's desk as our classroom empties. Ms. Brumby, my English teacher, always dresses in one color. The color of the day is brown. Today if she were a horse, she'd be a frizzy-maned Brumby, an Australian scrub horse. Brumbies, the horses, are bony, Roman-nosed, disagreeable, and hard to work with.

Ms. Brumby's small gray eyes squint as she bends over my English essay. When she looks up from her desk, she lets out a sigh that turns into a growl.

"Is it that bad?" I already told her why it was a day late. I lost my handwritten copy and had to recreate the paper from my notes. Since it was about horses, it wasn't too hard. Ms. Brumby and I are alone in the room, but I hear whispers in the hallway. I'll bet Summer and her herd are spying.

"Winnie, I was ready to believe you about your 'lost' paper." She makes finger quotes around "lost." I start to thank her, but she breaks in. "Let me finish. I *was* ready until it came to my attention that you have cheated."

"What?"

"Oh, you've made little changes here and there, but you haven't fooled me. You copied someone else's paper. The material and organization are the same. Parts are word for word from the other student's paper. It's your bad luck that the other teacher and I graded papers together, and I recognized her student's work as soon as you turned in this."

"But I didn't—!"

"Don't even try to talk your way out of this. I have proof, Winnie. You, of course, will fail this assignment." She folds a piece of paper and seals it in an envelope marked *Mr. and Mrs. Willis.* "Take this to your parents. I will need to speak with them."

She dismisses me without another word, and it all stinks. First, she called me a cheater. And second, this is the second year she's had me in class, and she doesn't even know my mom is dead.

I leave before she can see my tears. I avoid talking to anybody the rest of the day, skip lunch, and am first out when the buzzer sounds.

Barker catches up with me. "Winnie!"

I pretend I don't hear him.

He gets closer. "I just heard. Don't worry. I'll find out what's really going on."

I'm too embarrassed to say anything, but when I look back, Barker is giving me a thumbs-up. Tears come, even though I don't want them to. I manage to say, "Thanks" and hope he hears me.

I make it home and run straight to my room for my Treasure Verse from this morning.

The LORD your God is going ahead of you. He will fight for you, just as you saw him do in Egypt.
Deuteronomy 1:30

Dear God,

This morning when I glanced at my Treasure Verse and saw it was about Egypt, I didn't think that verse had anything to do with me. Now I do. Heavenly Father, I really need you to go to school ahead of me and fight for me. You're the only One who can know for sure I didn't cheat because you see everything. Would you mind talking to Dad before I give him this note that says his daughter is a cheater? I worked hard on that paper (twice!)

because I love talking about horses. I don't understand why Ms. Brumby would accuse me of cheating.

Lizzy's shouting that dinner's ready. I better go down and give the note to Dad.

Love, Winnie

Lizzy and Dad are talking over Lizzy's cheese dinner: baked shredded cheese, cheese potatoes, cheese bread. I sit down and hand Ms. Brumby's note to Dad.

He holds it up and squints at it. "Read it for me, will you? I left my glasses in the basement."

Lizzy does the honors, reading how I cheated and copied someone else's essay. She glances at me before finishing. "We do have proof and would like to meet with you both before school starts tomorrow."

"I didn't cheat, Dad." Salt water drowns my vocal cords, making me sound hoarser than usual. I hold my breath and wait for Dad to yell at me. When he slams down the note, I almost fall off my chair.

"Has this woman ever met you, Winnie?" Dad shouts, not waiting for an answer. "Anyone who has would never believe you'd cheat! Oh, I'll be there in the morning. That teacher is about to get a large mass of my cerebrum!"

"Could I come?" Lizzy asks, giving me a hug. "I'll tell them my sister never cheats!"

They leave the table at the same time, too fast for me to understand what just happened. To their backs, I shout, "Thank you!" but I mean so much more. They believe me.

I need time to think things through, which means I need Nickers. A waning moon shines a narrow pathway to the barn, where Nickers is munching hay next to Towaco. I hug my horse, smelling her scent like incense, like prayer. And the next thing I know, I am praying, thanking God for going ahead of me to my dad. *Please go ahead of me to Ms. Brumby too, Lord. Plus, I'm going to need you to do the last part of that verse and fight for me like you did in Egypt.*

To be continued . . .

Lassoing the Truth

Winnie was accused of something she didn't do, but she knew God understood what really happened. If you're ever falsely accused, you can go straight to God, who knows your heart and the truth about you. He is the Truth, and he's on your side.

Whoa!

Have you ever been accused of something you didn't do? Tell God what that felt like. How does it feel knowing God sees you and knows the truth about you? Journal to God about your belief and trust in him.

____

____

____

____

____

____

____

Dear God, thank you for always knowing the truth about me and for going ahead of me.

Giddyup!

Choose a color card that matches how you felt when accused of something you didn't do.

The LORD your God is going ahead of you. He will fight for you, just as you saw him do in Egypt.
Deuteronomy 1:30

Here's another great verse for your Treasure Box, a promise that God is on your side:

What shall we say about such wonderful things as these? If God is for us, who can ever be against us?
Romans 8:31

23

Truth Wins

Unfailing love and truth have met together. Righteousness and peace have kissed! Truth springs up from the earth, and righteousness smiles down from heaven.

Psalm 85:10-11

It's still dark outside when I give up on sleep. All night, pictures flashed through my mind: me standing at the teacher's desk; Ms. Brumby making finger quotes around "lost" paper; Summer and her herd spying, even though I only heard them whispering.

Around 5 a.m. I turn on my bedside light and pull out my Treasure Box. I choose a purple card, because I'm feeling anxious.

Unfailing love and truth have met together. Righteousness and peace have kissed! Truth springs up from the earth, and righteousness smiles down from heaven.

Psalm 85:10-11

Dear God,

Wow! Thank you for being the Truth and unfailing love! Sometimes it's hard to believe you could love me, but you do. Thanks for Jesus making it possible. No matter what happens today, you know the truth. So if Ms. Brumby is still frowning at me, I'll picture you smiling down from heaven.

I remember how Mom would thank you for answering what we'd just prayed for, before anything changed. Lizzy does it too now. So this is me trying to believe you've already got this morning covered and Ms. Brumby convinced. Thank you for this morning's meeting and making my teacher see the truth (even though it hasn't happened yet).

Love and Truth, Winnie

I hear Lizzy in the kitchen already, and I think I hear Dad too although they're keeping their voices low. God, Dad, and Lizzy believe me. So would Mom.

Dad, Lizzy, and I are first through the school doors. Dad takes my hand, and Lizzy holds my other hand. We let go before Dad and I enter the classroom. I feel like a yearling at her first horse show.

Ms. Brumby, dressed fancy from her orange hair ribbon to her orange high heels, hovers over a stack of papers. Dad doesn't wait for her to look up. "I am Mr. Willis. Mrs. Willis won't be joining us because she died in a terrible accident before we moved to Ashland. You've had my daughter in your classroom for quite some time. Apparently, you don't know Winnie at all. My daughter did not cheat! She turned in her own paper, and furthermore—!"

Ms. Brumby has been holding up her hand in a STOP gesture. Now she interrupts Dad. "Please, Mr. Willis. I agree with you." I don't think any other words could have stopped my dad. "I am so sorry Winnie lost her mother, and you your wife. It's a terrible admission to you that I didn't know. Please accept my apology." She turns to me with a face I've never seen her wear before. "I am really sorry, Winnie. I hope you'll forgive me."

Note to self: *I have just witnessed a miracle!*

Dad opens his mouth to speak, but Ms. Brumby says, "Please let me explain. It came to our attention—the other teacher and myself—that the paper turned in for a high school assignment, an essay on horses, was very similar to the one Winnie turned in late. We made the wrong assumption that Winnie had copied the other student's paper. Since I talked with Winnie, we have learned that the high schooler is the one who copied your *lost* paper."

"Which is what I told you. I had to rewrite the essay from my notes."

"And you were right," she admits. "Since the high school teacher gave the paper an A+, you'll be happy to know I've given you that grade as well."

Dad's tight lips and narrowed eyes tell me this information doesn't make him as happy as Ms. Brumby hopes. "Who stole Winnie's essay and lied about it?"

Ms. Brumby picks up her red pencil and studies it as

if she's never held one. "I'm sorry. I can't give you that information."

Behind us, someone clears his throat super loud. I turn to see Eddy Barker standing next to Lizzy in the doorway. "I can tell you," Barker says. "Robert Spidell."

Ms. Brumby looks away.

"I could have guessed," Dad says. "Thanks, Eddy. How did you find out?"

Barker grins. "Summer Spidell, Robert's sister—she told me."

I can't believe this. "Why would Summer tell the truth to help me?"

Kids are trailing in. Summer takes her seat. "What's going on?" she asks.

Still amazed, I walk over to her. "Barker told us what you did. Thanks, Summer."

Summer's face scrunches up like she's stepped in a pile of manure. "Don't get the wrong idea. I was just getting even with my brother for snitching on me. You know me, Winnie. If I ever so much as lifted a finger to help you, I'd never show my face around here again."

Note to self: *Encourage Summer to lift her finger.*

We're halfway through English when today's verse—at least, part of it, flashes through my brain. *Truth springs up from the earth, and righteousness smiles down from heaven.* Truth can spring from weird places when God goes ahead of us, I guess—from the earth, and even from Summer Spidell.

Note to self: *On second thought, I guess Summer's finger can stay where it is.*

Lassoing the Truth

Winnie didn't know if her teacher would still refuse to believe her, but she knew God was with her. And she trusted that he would bring out the truth. If you're ever falsely accused, you can, and should, talk to the accuser and explain the truth. But the best first step is to pour out your heart to God and trust him to bring out the truth. He is Truth!

Whoa!

Journal what today's verse means to you: God's unfailing love, peace, and truth; truth springing up and righteousness smiling down from heaven. Share details with God about how you sense his love and truth.

____

____

____

____

____

____

____

____

____

Dear God, thank you for caring so much about me. Thank you for your unfailing love and truth.

Giddyup!

Fill a purple card with today's verse.

Unfailing love and truth have met together. Righteousness and peace have kissed! Truth springs up from the earth, and righteousness smiles down from heaven.

Psalm 85:10-11

Write this New Testament verse on a green card:

The Word became flesh and made his dwelling among us. We have seen his glory, the glory of the one and only Son, who came from the Father, full of grace and truth.

John 1:14, NIV

This is the day the L*ORD has made.*
We will rejoice and be glad in it.

Psalm 118:24

Once again, it's dark when I wake up, and I can't get back to sleep. Instead of fighting it, I drag out my Treasure Box and choose a green (joyful) card. Why not?

This is the day the LORD has made.
We will rejoice and be glad in it.
Psalm 118:24

Dear God,

This verse sounds like being happy today is a choice. And so, I choose happy. I am declaring today a Joy Day! You went to all the trouble of making this day (even though it's a school day). The least I can do is rejoice in it.

I feel like this is a great idea, but I know I can't pull it off without you. Pretty exciting!

Love, Joyful Winnie (If my name were Jenny,
I could be Joyful Jenny—ha!)

For breakfast, Lizzy's made blackberry pancakes in the shape of lizards. She's whistling an old hymn neither of us can name. "I've got it," I say after a dozen wrong guesses between us. "It's 'Lizard Lullaby' or 'Freedom Frog.'" We laugh so loud we wake up Dad. He joins us and smiles more than I can remember. Then he hums our tune while he eats pancakes with his battery-operated fork.

Like always, I do barn chores before school. But instead of regretting that I can't just stay with the horses and not go to school, I whisper to Nickers, "Rejoice today, my wonderful horse." It's too cold to walk or bike to school, so we take the bus. Through the frosty bus window, I watch pines pass in shades of green. I thank God for not creating everything in black and white, like old movies on TV. I keep thanking God for Nickers, for Jesus sitting here with me, and for Lizzy sitting with us. Gray clouds gather behind the bus as if chasing us.

Note to self: *God made today. Great job, God!*

Even a Joy Day has rough patches, right? Mr. Lee makes us run laps in gym because Summer's herd kept talking when he tried to get their attention. I feel like shoving Summer as I run past her. But I imagine Jesus running beside me, and the image of the three of us is so funny that I have to choke down laughter so I won't get us all in trouble again.

In pre-algebra, I feel dumber than a boot full of rocks and wonder if I'll ever have to use this stuff in real life. But I choose to listen to God's whisper: *Hey! I made this day, Winnie. Find my joy in it.* Or something like that. Then I glance out the window and see two of Catman's cats waiting for him in the evergreen bushes.

Right in computer class when I'm confused and the joy starts leaking out of me like air from a stabbed balloon, I hear the winds and the branches scratching at the window, eager to get in. I smile inside at God, who made this day to rejoice in (not to complain about).

At home, it's so easy to rejoice, especially in the barn, even though one of the Mustangs refuses to work in the wind. When Mason comes to see the filly he named Buddy, he makes me smile with his smile. "Hey, buddy!" I call.

He frowns at me, and I realize he thinks I'm greeting his horse, Buddy. "Sorry, Mason. I was calling you buddy, as in my buddy. I mean, the real Buddy is yours, and I—never mind." I watch him take off his mittens and try to pull them over Buddy's ears until I come to Buddy's rescue.

After Mason leaves, I still have time to finish with a joy ride on Nickers before studying algebra. I whistle for my horse. She whinnies and runs toward me at a dead gallop, sliding to a stop only when close enough for me to swing up on her back. Taking a handful of mane, I lean forward and whisper, "Canter." She canters from a standstill, circling the pasture, following the pressure of my legs, changing directions and leads, her hooves barely touching the ground. Around us, trees breathe applause to the One who made them. I ride with pure joy, imagining Jesus riding double with me while bear-shaped clouds flatten to dance above the sun before being slowly swallowed by earth.

Back in the barn, I wrap my arms around Nickers, pressing my cheek to her neck, content with the scent of horse and the joy of the Lord.

In my bedroom, I pull out my Treasure Box and have a sudden urge to read as many green cards as I can before falling asleep. There are so many good ones!

I am overwhelmed with joy in the LORD my God!
Isaiah 61:10

Let the godly rejoice. Let them be glad in God's presence. Let them be filled with joy.
Psalm 68:3

You will show me the way of life, granting me the joy of your presence and the pleasures of living with you forever.

Psalm 16:11

Always be full of joy in the Lord. I say it again—rejoice!

Philippians 4:4

The last thing I remember is hearing "Amen." I think it came from me.

Lassoing the Truth

Reasons for joy are all around us. Like Winnie, we should be continually amazed at God's creation. Often, being filled with wonder is choosing to pay attention and be grateful. Or, we can walk right past God's daily gifts without noticing them. God promises us a lifetime of joy in him if we choose joy.

Whoa!

What do you think "joy in the Lord" really means? Journal about joy! Write about what makes you joyful and why. Share details about a specific experience or observation.

____

____

____

____

____

____

____

God, thank you for giving me so many ways to experience your joy. Please help me be amazed at what you've done.

Giddyup!

Copy today's verse onto a green card.

This is the day the LORD has made.
We will rejoice and be glad in it.
Psalm 118:24

In today's devotional, you're given several verses, all about joy. Copy a few on green cards for your Treasure Box.

I am overwhelmed with joy in the LORD my God!
Isaiah 61:10

Let the godly rejoice. Let them be glad in God's presence. Let them be filled with joy.

Psalm 68:3

You will show me the way of life, granting me the joy of your presence and the pleasures of living with you forever.

Psalm 16:11

Always be full of joy in the Lord. I say it again—rejoice!

Philippians 4:4

25

Sincere Fear

I praise God for what he has promised. I trust in God, so why should I be afraid? What can mere mortals do to me?

Psalm 56:4

Dad and Lizzy are still asleep when I walk to the barn to check on Hero, the wannabe trail-riding standardbred the Cyders dropped off last week. Mrs. Cyders confessed she's "a little frightened" of horses, which is weird since they run a campground with trail rides and boat rentals.

Note to self: *Wonder if she's afraid of canoes?*

I'm supposed to gentle Hero so anybody can ride him. But right now, I wouldn't let anybody near him. Yesterday, Hero reared when a caterpillar crossed the road in front of us. When a train whistle blew a mile away, the horse bolted. Taking him on trails in the woods feels like riding through the fun house where Mom took Lizzy and me and something jumped out around every corner, making us scream our heads off. Hero had a fit and bucked when a branch cracked on a poplar. That horse is scared of his own shadow.

At least Mario, the Hathaways' horse, is doing great in horse shows. Compared to the terrified Hero, though, Mario's *fear* was more like shyness.

I finish chores and drop a small salt block into Hero's trough. The scaredy-cat horse races out of the barn, leaving Buddy shaking with fright. *Thanks a lot, Hero.* I have to stay with the little filly and calm her down.

"Winnie! The bus is here!" Lizzy sounds out of breath.

"Go. I'll ride my bike." *And be late to class . . . again.*

Note to self: *This is Hero's fault.*

At school and out of breath, I shove my bike into the rack and notice that the gym door looks like it didn't close right, something that's happened before. My homeroom is next to the gym. It's starting to sleet. If I can get inside . . .

In seconds I'm crossing the empty gym and sliding into my back-row seat as kids open their workbooks. My teacher hasn't looked up from his desk. Nobody's turned around. Nobody saw me. I'm home free!

"Attention!"

I jump at the loudspeaker blaring.

Our principal talks so loud he doesn't need a speaker. **"Intruder in the building! Warning!"**

We've had intruder drills before, but they always warn us first. Our class springs into action. Barker turns the special lock on the classroom door, while Sal and Brianna pull down black shades over our windows. Four guys shove desks against the door. Last year we all hid in different places, but now we hide together. Kids are clustered in the corner already.

"Winnie!" Barker takes my elbow and pulls me out of my desk. "Come on!"

Dazed, I follow Barker to the corner, and he sits in front of me. I'm shivering, but I feel hot. Note to self: *Don't be stupid. This is a drill.*

But why didn't the principal announce we'd be having an intruder drill?

Summer, who's sitting behind me, using me as a shield, leans up and whispers, "This is no drill, Winnie. This is for real."

I think I might throw up. My heart beats like galloping horses' hooves.

"Winnie, are you okay?" Barker is standing over me. "You knew it was just a drill, right? You heard the principal warn us at the start of class."

I didn't hear the announcement because I wasn't in the classroom. Barker jogs to the door and unlocks it. The screech of moving desks mixes with laughter. Sunshine pours in through the windows now.

This was just a drill. I get up and find my desk. Just a drill. Not real.

Note to self: *But it could have been.*

As soon as I'm home, I run to the pasture to hug Nickers. Before I reach her, she nickers at me. We run to each other, like lovers in an old movie. I breathe in horse, the best smell in the world. Swinging to her back, I whisper, "I love you, Nickers!" Then we ride and ride. I feel grateful to God for my horse, for feeling free and safe . . . until I swing off and my feet touch the ground. Then my heart shivers in the darkening drizzle as I run to the house.

Before climbing into bed, I pull out a purple card from the scared file.

I praise God for what he has promised. I trust in God, so why should I be afraid? What can mere mortals do to me?

Psalm 56:4

Dear God,

I really wish I'd trusted you when I got so scared at school today. All I could think of was the intruder who wasn't even there. I didn't think about you or talk to you at all.

Thanks for giving me the perfect verse. You're right. Why should I be afraid? You're greater than anyone. What could an old intruder do to me anyway? I'll memorize this verse, and maybe it can help me get Hero over his fears too.

Thanks again. Love, Winnie

I reread the Treasure Verse, letting the words sink into my quivering brain, when something creaks. It's on the stairs. It stops.

But someone's in the kitchen. A door opens. Closes. I think about shouting to see if it's Dad. But my throat is too dry. There's a steady scratching at my window as if someone's trying to open it from the outside. In the next minute, I hear Lizzy in the kitchen, praying out loud on her way to bed.

I jump in bed and look over at the window, where branches are scratching the windowpane. Still, I pull the covers over my head and pray for sleep.

To be continued . . .

Lassoing the Truth

Like Winnie, you probably know what it feels like to be afraid. Some fears sound silly (like vampires in your closet), but other fears are grounded in real dangers. If you have fears, real or imagined, you can tell your Father in heaven. Reach out to the all-powerful God.

Whoa!

Journal honestly about any fears you have or have had in the past. What did it feel like the last time you were truly afraid? Journal your answer to the psalmist's questions in today's verse: *I trust in God, so why should I be afraid? What can mere mortals do to me?*

Dear God, sometimes my fears can trap me and take over everything else, like peace and hope. Please remind me that I'm always with you, no matter where I go.

Giddyup!

Make a new purple card with today's verse on it.

I praise God for what he has promised. I trust in God, so why should I be afraid? What can mere mortals do to me?
Psalm 56:4

If your fears are keeping you awake or taking up too much space in your head, talk to God and tell your parents. Don't keep your fears secret.

26

Perfect Love

There is no fear in love. But perfect love drives out fear, because fear has to do with punishment. The one who fears is not made perfect in love.

1 John 4:18, NIV

My bedside clock reads 4:03 when I jerk myself awake. I was in the middle of a bad dream, and there's no way I'm going back to sleep and finishing it. When I roll out of bed, my foot lands on what turns out to be a Treasure Verse card. It must have fallen out of my Treasure Box last night. I pick it up and turn on my lamp to read. It's a purple card.

In peace I will lie down and sleep, for you alone,
O LORD, will keep me safe.
Psalm 4:8

Note to self: *Why didn't I read this before I went to bed?*

It's funny, and I even laugh thinking about how I stepped on this free-falling card. But the laugh doesn't last. Not like the fear. In the night, I kept hearing the loudspeaker from the school drill: "Intruder alert!"

I need to start working with Hero on *his* fears, but I don't know what else to do. I've tried everything I can think of, and he's still afraid of every little thing. Note to self: *Like someone else I know.* Maybe the horse just doesn't like me. Truth is, I'm not that crazy about him.

Instead of heading for the barn, I reach for my Treasure Box and take out another purple card.

There is no fear in love. But perfect love drives out fear, because fear has to do with punishment. The one who fears is not made perfect in love.

1 John 4:18, NIV

I get my journal, plop on the floor cross-legged, and write.

Dear God,

How do you know exactly what I need? "Perfect love drives out fear." I know you love me perfectly, but I didn't even ask you to help me or protect me at school yesterday. It was like fear took over my mind, heart, and body. What if I'd looked to you instead of looking for an intruder?

I'm still not sure I understand the entire verse, but I love the part about perfect love getting rid of fear. I know how much you love me. I'll try to think of that the next time I'm scared. And Hero's fear? Poor Hero hasn't felt perfect love, or much love at all, not from me. Will you help me love Hero and show him your perfect love?

Thank you, Jesus, for perfect love!

Love, Winnie

Outside a half-sun pushes through low clouds, turning them burnt orange and red. I'd love a horse blanket that color. My nose hairs tickle, and my breath sends mouth clouds that disappear.

All the horses are in the barn, stirring and nickering thanks for their early breakfast. Nickers and I exchange our Navajo greeting as I blow gently into her nostrils. Sometimes I ache with how much I love her.

Clump! A loud noise comes from the end stall. The barn is a perfect place for an intruder to hide. *Perfect.* Right.

God loves me with perfect love. I don't need to be afraid. The barn might be a good hideout for an intruder, but more likely, the ornery Mustangs are in a shoving match. I check, and I'm right. No intruders. No fear. Just young Mustangs. *Perfect love drives out fear.*

Hero turns wide eyes on me when I slip into his stall, keeping away from his backside, leaving distance between him and the sides of the stall. "Hey, boy." I scratch his chest, his "special scratching spot," until I feel his muscles relax. I stroke him all over, whispering, "Hero, I'm sorry we haven't gotten along very well. But I get it, about being afraid. And I do love you, even if you haven't felt it, even if *I* haven't felt it. My love can never be perfect like God's. But I want you to know you're loved. We'll get through this together."

After taking extra care with Hero's grooming in the cross ties, I saddle him, then lead him around the pasture. A sparrow flies in front of me, and Hero shies, tugging me off my feet. Planting a smile on my face, I stroke his neck. "It's okay, Hero. No fear. I love you."

The gelding shies again, thanks to a squirrel chittering from a tree. And again, when Towaco races along the fence. And again, when a flock of blackbirds takes off near us. Each time, I tell Hero that I love him. And the funny thing is I'm meaning it more and more.

After a break, I mount him, and we ride in the round pen, then in the pasture. He rears when a dog barks and bucks when a Mustang gets too close. But the longer we ride, the more I love on him, the better the ride, the fewer the fears . . . for both of us.

At the end of the day when I climb under the covers, I talk to Jesus. *Thanks for loving me. Please help me love Hero enough that he'll get over his fears. I think I'm learning how powerful your perfect love is. Fear really doesn't stand a chance.*

I close my eyes and have a feeling I'm about to get a good night's sleep.

Lassoing the Truth

When Winnie was frightened, fear took over, and she looked for danger in every corner. She couldn't get rid of her fear until God showed her that fear is no match for God's perfect love. Like Winnie, you may experience fear that grabs you and won't let go. But perfect love is stronger. The Bible reveals God's powerful, unfailing, perfect love. Remember that wherever fear lurks, the perfect love of Christ can get rid of it.

Whoa!

If you've had an ongoing fear, what did you do to try to get over it? Have you felt Jesus' perfect love? Journal to God and thank him for his perfect love. Describe what "perfect love" means to you and how trusting God's love could help when you're afraid.

Dear God, thank you for loving me so much that you died for me. Please help me cling to you when I'm afraid.

Giddyup!

Copy today's verse onto a purple card.

There is no fear in love. But perfect love drives out fear, because fear has to do with punishment. The one who fears is not made perfect in love.

1 John 4:18, NIV

If you like, copy Winnie's bonus verse, Psalm 4:8, on another purple card.

In peace I will lie down and sleep, for you alone, O LORD, will keep me safe.

Psalm 4:8

27

Worthy of Praise

Let them praise the Lord *for his great love and for the wonderful things he has done for them.*

Psalm 107:15

Even though it's Sunday and Pastor Ralph will give us a bunch of Scriptures, I'm pulling out my Treasure Box and choosing a green card.

Let them praise the Lord for his great love and for the wonderful things he has done for them.

Psalm 107:15

Dear God,

I should be praising you more! You've done wonderful things for me. And I love your "great love." But you know what? I'm not sure I know how to praise. I mean, I thank you a lot—not enough, I know. And I have Joy Days sometimes. But praise? I'm not good at that, and I don't know if I ever do it.

Would you mind showing me how to praise you? Sometimes I—

Mr. Barker is outside honking the Barker Bus. Time for church!

Love, Winnie the Poor Praiser

I love standing in our church pew and singing hymns that Pastor Ralph calls "Songs of Praise." M moves to stand beside Lizzy, the singer in the Willis family. Still, I feel like I'm praising God when we sing in church. But how can I praise the rest of the week? Even *I'm* not a fan of my singing.

Sunday afternoon I sit on my bed and read a bunch of psalms because Lizzy told me they're really songs. I reread my Treasure Verse and write in my journal: *Praise the Lord for his great love.* I start listing "The Wonderful Things He Has Done for Me":

* Giving me—for a time—Mom, the best horse gentler in the world
* Dad, who works hard and loves me

* Lizzy, the best sister in the world
* Nickers!

After dinner, I add to my list. It grows so long that I stay up way past bedtime. When I read over my whole list, I really am thankful. But is that praise?

I praise you for my warm socks. I'm walking into school on Monday morning and trying to praise. I guess I'm thankful for my socks, but it doesn't feel like praise.

All day at school I try. *Praise be to you for my peanut-butter-and-honey sandwich and the sister who made it. I praise you for helping me not miss more math problems than I got right. Praise and hallelujah that I don't have to sit next to Summer in English class.*

Lizzy takes the bus home, but I wait for Catman and M. The oak tree in the school lawn is hanging on to its wrinkled brown leaves. I sniff the chilled air.

"Something groovy in the air?" Catman is the sneakiest person in the world, though not on purpose. M is second.

"I love the smell of pines." I grin at them, M dressed in head-to-toe black, Catman in his camo jacket and green bell-bottoms. *God, you did a great job making these guys.*

Catman picks up Aussie, who rarely leaves the Coolidge grounds. We start walking, and I end up telling M and Catman my problem with praising God. When we reach my house, I've talked the whole way. "Thanks for listening. I guess I'll have to wait for Sunday to praise."

Catman starts for the shortcut home, then turns back. "Liking the smell of pines sounds like praise to me."

"Right." I'm skeptical.

M is still following me although his house is in the opposite direction. We go into my kitchen, and Lizzy gives us hot chocolate. "Thanks for the chocolate and the steam it makes," Lizzy prays.

When I go to the barn to work the horses, M tags along and takes Catman's spectator spot on the fence. First, I ride Hawk's horse, Towaco, since he's restless and gets wound up with the chilly wind. After a short ride and a few bucks for good measure, he settles in. "There you go! Good job, Towaco! Look at what you did—perfect lead changes! I love you, Appy."

M applauds. Next, I bring out the Morgan mare the Johnsons plan to give their daughter for her birthday. I've been working Black Beauty on the ground, but today I'm riding her with the Western saddle. We start off rocky, with Beauty sidestepping and fussing as soon as I'm on her back. "Good girl! You're letting me ride!"

The sun is fading as we leave the round pen, but the mare is following commands. M walks beside us to the barn. "M, wasn't Beauty wonderful?"

M reaches up and strokes Beauty's mane. "True. But I think you've praised those horses enough for both of us." He twitches his eyebrows, then walks off.

Did I praise them? All I did was tell them how great they really are.

Something inside me lifts, or maybe parts, like Moses' path through the Red Sea. "Wow! God! Only you could use M to help me understand praise! How kind and caring you are to me! I love your sense of humor, Lord!"

I think I've been praying out loud, like Lizzy, but I'm not sure. I step out of the barn, surprised to see the Big Dipper and Orion under a slice of moon. "How could I worry about giving you praise when you've created praise-worthy stuff everywhere I look?"

I glance both ways to make sure I'm alone with God. Then I look up and shout, "Praise the Lord!"

Lassoing the Truth

Winnie discovered that praising God is noticing the amazing things God has done, and is still doing—then telling God how amazed you are at his workmanship. Like Winnie in this story, you don't have to use fancy words and be solemn and serious. Praise comes naturally when we take time to notice all God has done, and is doing, for us.

In your journal, make a list of wonderful things God has done for you. Where has God done a superb job? You might take a walk with your journal and record a few of God's praiseworthy wonders.

Dear God, please help me to praise you more, to notice everything you're doing. Thanks for being so worthy of praise!

Giddyup!

Write today's verse on a green card.

Let them praise the LORD for his great love and for the wonderful things he has done for them.

Psalm 107:15

List five "wonderful things" God has done for you, and praise him for each one. Share a couple of them with a parent or friend.

28

Together

*Let us not neglect our meeting together, as some people do,
but encourage one another, especially now that
the day of his return is drawing near.*

Hebrews 10:25

This morning at church, Pastor Ralph said something that really made me think—not that he doesn't usually. If I don't get it, it's my fault for thinking of other stuff while he's giving his sermon. Anyway, he said that God made us with five physical senses: sight, hearing, smell, taste, and touch. I already knew that from science. But he said God made us with the same five spiritual senses so we can know him better. That kind of makes sense, I guess. (No pun intended.) But I don't get how that would work.

Catman and M catch me on the way out of church.

"Hey, cats!" Catman calls. "Up for back-bike cruising?"

"I'm down with that," M answers. His church bulletin has been torn in the shape of an ear. "I'll see if Barker wants to join."

"Winifred?" Catman's head tilts down to my level.

"Sounds like fun, Calvin. Thanks for asking. But I need some alone time to find out about this spiritual-senses stuff."

"Hmmm," Catman says. "More alone time? You've claimed a lot of that lately."

I start to object but realize he's right. Lately, I haven't had much time to play or hang out. I've been fine on my own.

M returns. "Barker will meet up with us on his frontward bike." He turns to me. "You out again?"

"Exactamundo," Catman answers for me. "What's the skinny, Winnie?"

I guess I have sort of been keeping to myself lately. "Next time. Have fun, guys."

After a bowl of oatmeal for lunch, I camp out on my bed and search for a verse that will explain spiritual hearing, or sight, or taste, or touch, or smell. I come up empty.

Note to self: *When in doubt, time for a Treasure Verse.*

I choose a yellow card because this spiritual senses thing confuses me.

> Let us not neglect our meeting together, as some people do, but encourage one another, especially now that the day of his return is drawing near.
>
> Hebrews 10:25

Maybe Mom put this card in the wrong place. It's a great verse—just not what I was hoping for. I've already "met together" in church. What I wanted was a spiritual-senses verse.

Hopefully, a ride on Nickers will make my brain kick in.

Nickers stops grazing when she sees me. She tosses her elegant head, sending her thick white mane flying. We both trot to meet in the middle of the super-green pasture. My heart whispers, *Thank you* at the sight of my horse, and I wonder again what spiritual sight means.

Or what about spiritual hearing? I can get chills when I hear my horse nicker, or mourning doves calling to heaven, or whip-poor-wills crying out their name. Or maybe spiritual hearing only happens when we read the Bible and hear the Word?

Nickers lowers her head for me to slip on her hackamore. I want to guide her around the pasture to check on the other horses. I take a fistful of mane and swing up on her back.

Nickers steps out, eager to take a trail through the woods, but I keep us in the pasture. We ride to Palo and Mino, the Palomino team I'm getting parade-ready so they won't get spooked by flags and tubas and crowds. The whole pasture smells like sunshine and horse today.

Heavenly Father, how am I going to recognize spiritual scent when I smell it?

We reach Buddy, Mason's little filly. I finger the white whorl on her blaze and the sunshine warmth of her back. Is spiritual touch like this? No, that's crazy.

The last sense is taste. I laugh because I've said to myself that Nickers is so sweet I could eat her up. Not really. *How does spiritual taste work, God?*

The rest of the afternoon, I ride each horse in the stable, except Buddy because she's too young. As I leave the barn, the sun hovers at the horizon with flat clouds, yellow in the center, coral on both sides. Pinkish clouds spread across the sky like cotton candy. I stop at our lilac bush and inhale. My mind pops up a photo of Mom spraying perfume before we left for church. She'd spray in front of herself, then step into the lilac-smelling air.

Back in my room, still wondering about spiritual senses, I keep thinking of Mom. She'd know all about spiritual senses. I can't figure it out on my own.

I dig for my Treasure Verse and read it again:

Let us not neglect our meeting together, as some people do, but encourage one another, especially now that the day of his return is drawing near.
Hebrews 10:25

Dear God,

It's taken me a while, but I think I'm starting to understand this verse. You were answering me, and I kept looking for answers on my own. The Treasure Verse was just what I needed all along. Of course, you're right! I have been neglecting meeting—not in church, but with the friends you've given me. Sometimes I think Nickers and I would be fine on our own. But I know keeping to myself isn't always a good thing. I need my friends. Maybe together, with your help, and Lizzy's, we can discover more about what Pastor Ralph called "spiritual senses." And even if we don't end up understanding everything, we can "encourage one another."

I'll stop writing now. I have some friends to invite for an encouraging meeting.

Love, Winnie

To be continued . . .

Lassoing the Truth

Winnie is so independent and content being a horse gentler that she subtly pulled away from her friends. As much as some of us enjoy being on our own, we do need each other. If you avoid groups of friends or if you're a loner, don't neglect the friends God places in your life. They may need your encouragement too.

Whoa!

The right friends can be a gift. Journal to God about your circle of friends, especially the people in your life who encourage you and help you as you all grow in Christ. Ask God what you can do to encourage a friend or friends.

____

____

____

____

____

____

____

Dear God, thank you for all the people in my life who love you and love me too. Help me encourage them in your name.

Giddyup!

Choose two cards (the color is up to you) and copy today's verse and another verse about encouraging each other.

Let us not neglect our meeting together, as some people do, but encourage one another, especially now that the day of his return is drawing near.
Hebrews 10:25

Encourage each other and build each other up, just as you are already doing.
1 Thessalonians 5:11

Ask God to remind you of a friend who might need encouragement. Call that person and talk or see about reconnecting with your friend.

29

Making Spiritual Sense

Taste and see that the Lord is good. Oh, the joys of those who take refuge in him!

Psalm 34:8

Dear God,

Thanks for encouraging me to get my friends together to figure out spiritual senses.

Catman, M, Barker, and Lizzy all said, "Yes!" Actually, Catman said, "Lay it on me," and M shouted, "Rock on!" Plus, Hawk said she'd come if her mom doesn't have plans for her. And thanks for my Treasure Verse today:

Taste and see that the Lord is good. Oh, the joys of those who take refuge in him!

Psalm 34:8

My friends and I are going to "taste and see that the Lord is good." I gave each friend a sense and asked them to bring a Bible verse about it. We're dedicating our Moon Check night to sharing what we've come up with.

Love, Winnie

I'm so eager for Moon Check that the sun is still up when I set out watch blankets. I use the time to groom Nickers, then Towaco, the Palominos, a Clydesdale I'm boarding, and little Buddy.

As I untangle manes and curry off mud, I think about the first Moon Check. Catman raced from the barn like it was on fire, crying, "Far out!" He grabbed a horse blanket and my hand and pulled me to the top of the hill. As the full moon climbed in a purple-black sky, we didn't say a word.

Then Catman whispered, "You have to scope out the moon, Winnie. Chill long enough to freak out over the orb." Since then, we do Moon Checks once a week. When M joined us, Catman pointed out stars and constellations. M loves Cassiopeia and claims the W-shaped constellation is an upside-down M.

"What's happening?" Catman appears with his quiet cat, Cat Burglar, Burg for short.

We climb the hill for the watch. I guess we don't exchange many words until the others trail up, but it feels like I've had a deep talk with Catman.

Barker settles behind me, next to M, who's dressed

in black and hard to see. "I've been at Pat's Pets," Barker explains. "Pat's coming after she closes."

I love Pat. "This will be her first Moon Check. Hawk's too, if she comes."

Lizzy springs up the hill with a plate of lemon-chocolate cookies, some round, some crescent-shaped, some curved strips. "They're moon-shaped!" she explains, passing the cookies around. "So, who goes first?"

M holds up a flower-shaped sandwich. "God gave us regular smell and created flowers for us to smell. Spiritual smell may be like incense. Second Corinthians 2:15 says, 'Our lives are a Christ-like fragrance rising up to God.' I picture Jesus watching out for our Christ-like smell."

Lizzy says, "That's awesome, M!" Then to God, "Thank you for the smell of a wet lizard and fresh bread." Back to us: "Winnie gave me taste because she says I'm a creative cook. I—"

Pat Haven stumbles up and sort of falls onto our blanket. "I'm blind as a bat, no offense."

We all welcome her to Moon Check, and then Lizzy continues, "Here's my verse: 'Taste and see that the LORD is good. Oh, the joys of those who take refuge in him!' Psalm 34:8. All people need to do is try Jesus. They'll see he's our loving Savior. Same goes for creative cooking. You—"

"My turn," Barker says, gracefully interrupting my chatty sister. "When I blow my dog whistle, my dogs come running. But people don't hear it. I think that's like the Good News of Christ and the teachings in the Bible being announced, but many people don't hear it. The message is there, but they're not listening. We can be spiritually deaf too, right? Like when we read something from the Bible, but it doesn't stick because we're really thinking about other things. Jesus said in Matthew 11:15, 'Anyone with ears to hear should listen and understand.' Maybe not paying attention to what Jesus says is spiritual deafness."

We stare at the moon, higher now. I'm thinking about how I can read a Treasure Verse and not think about it again, probably because I don't want to do what it says.

Catman gazes at the moon. "Cats' eyes are outta sight in moonlight! They're seeing groovier than we are right now, watching tiny creatures scurry by, unseen by our eyes. Second Corinthians 4:18 says, 'We fix our gaze on things that cannot be seen. For the things we see now will soon be gone, but the things we cannot see will last forever.'"

"Heavy," M says. "Spiritual sight."

Catman holds up Burg for a better view of the moon. "Do your thing, Winnie."

"I thought touch would be easy—which is why I kept it for myself. A couple of you have helped me imprint foals. The goal is to touch the foal all over until he relaxes and enjoys your touch. That's what I think God wants from us—to let him touch us and be at home in our hearts.

"I tried to memorize Luke 4:40. 'As the sun went down that evening, people throughout the village brought sick family members to Jesus. No matter what their diseases were, the touch of his hand healed every one.' I found lots of verses about being touched by Jesus, holding his hand, resting your head on his shoulder, being carried in his arms. But I couldn't memorize all of them."

Silence surrounds us in our semicircle under the moon. Then I think I hear Dad's laugh. I turn around, and way in the back are Hawk and Dad. I run over and hug them. "Thanks for showing up. I guess we're done, though."

"I do not think so," Hawk says.

"Hawk and I have an idea," Dad says. "We're surprised you didn't think of it yourself."

To be continued . . .

Lassoing the Truth

With the help of her friends, Winnie began to understand "spiritual senses" and how they can help her draw closer to God. Hopefully, you, too, want to grow in your relationship with God. God has given us many ways to deepen our relationship with him, including the use of our spiritual senses.

Whoa!

How would you describe your relationship with God through Jesus? Are you as close to God as you'd like to be? Journal honestly with God about your friendship and desire to grow. How could you draw closer to God every day through your spiritual senses?

Dear God, please help me grow more aware of what you're doing in the world and in me.

Giddyup!

Pick as many verses as you like and write each on a different card. Fill that Treasure Box!

Taste and see that the LORD is good. Oh, the joys of those who take refuge in him!

Psalm 34:8

Our lives are a Christ-like fragrance rising up to God.

2 Corinthians 2:15

Anyone with ears to hear should listen and understand.

Matthew 11:15

We fix our gaze on things that cannot be seen.

2 Corinthians 4:18

As the sun went down that evening, people throughout the village brought sick family members to Jesus. No matter what their diseases were, the touch of his hand healed every one.

Luke 4:40

30

Riding the Moon

Sing to the one who rides across the ancient heavens,
his mighty voice thundering from the sky.

Psalm 68:33

"Moon Ride!" Dad and Hawk shout as if they've practiced this.

"Far out!" I exclaim. I can't believe I didn't think of ending our Moon Check with a horse ride.

Everybody talks at once as I lead the way to the barn. My mind is whirling, trying to match horses and riders. "Catman! M! Hawk! Let's saddle some horses!"

We run out of Western saddles. Hawk uses her English saddle, and Nickers is fine bareback. We use an old Army saddle on Clyde the Clydesdale. "Catman?" I don't see him . . . until he flashes the peace sign from the back of Nickers. Works for me.

After some wrangling, here's the matchup:

Dad and Lizzy on Clyde. Lizzy looks glued to Dad's back. I do a double take, since Lizzy has always refused to ride. And if Dad ever rode, I've never seen it.

Hawk and Barker on Towaco, Barker looking like he'd rather ride a dog.

M mounts Palo but looks lonely up there.

Madeline and Mason walk into the barn, looking confused. "What's going on?" Madeline asks.

Mason races to his horse. "Ride Buddy! Me!"

Madeline gasps.

I squat down with Buddy and Mason. "Mason, Buddy needs to grow a little more." I can't stand seeing his big eyes fill with tears. "Madeline, would you let Mason ride with one of us? Please?"

She lifts Mason up, and I think she plans to carry him away. Instead, she sighs. "Who would you like to ride with, Mason?"

Mason squirms out of her arms and runs to M, who says, "Little M! Want to see a giant M in the sky?" He reaches down and, practically upside down, hoists Mason up and sets him in front. He wraps Mason's fingers around the saddlehorn. "Don't let go, my man."

"Everybody, hold your horses! No offense. Which cow pony is mine?" Pat has told me stories of her cowgirl life, but I've never seen her ride.

"How about the other Palomino?" I take her to the bigger horse and shorten the stirrups. "This is Mino. M and Mason have Palo."

Pat takes the reins. "Palo and Mino. Palomino! If that's not the bee's knees! No offense."

I glance over to Dad and Lizzy. "You sure you two are okay?"

"I'm lonely as a badger up here. No offense." Pat told me once that badgers don't like company. "You! Madeline Edison! Come onboard."

Madeline makes a choking sound, and I try to rescue her from Pat. "Pat, Madeline's letting Mason ride. But she's not really a fan of horses."

"Me either!" Lizzy says, as Clyde starts heading for the pasture on his own.

"Stuff and nonsense!" Pat says. "I'll meet you at the mounting block, Maddie!"

Nickers leads the way as light gray clouds sweep across the moon, then keep on going, leaving moonshine so bright I can see every blade of grass. We form a natural line exiting the barn, stepping onto a moonbeam that serves as a red carpet. I twist around to peer past Catman at the faces of Hawk and Barker on Towaco, who dances in place behind Pat and Madeline. Two women couldn't be more different, but as Palo trots, they bounce in unison. Buddy watches from the center of our circle, looking like a four-legged ringmaster.

I can't see Catman's face, but I imagine him smiling up at the moon, wrapped in moonlight, one arm raised with the peace sign, the other hugging my waist.

"Dear God, thank you! I praise you for the touch of a friend and for your hand holding me and guiding me. Thanks for the smell of horse, for the whickers and snorts I hear, for the sight of your moon, your eternal and faithful witness in the sky."

"I like your prayer, Winnie," Lizzy calls. "Don't forget the taste of the wind!"

Note to self: *I was praying out loud?*

I stick out my tongue for the pine-scented air and spot Pat and Madeline doing the same.

Dad and Lizzy laugh, looking less skeleton-stiff.

I want to breathe it all in. *Lord, please take a picture of this moment.* A hint of sadness brushes my heart. This moment would be perfect if Mom were here. She'd cheer for Dad and Lizzy on a horse for sure. *Thank you for my mom.*

Catman rests his chin on my head. A wave of blond hair blows across my cheek. "Hang tight, Winnie. You'll see her again." I don't know how he knows, but he always knows.

I shift so I can see his face. "Catman, I don't want to lose this." *Him. Dad, Lizzy, everybody.* "I get scared, or sad sometimes, thinking about what's ahead. There could be a war, or a horrible disease, or a depression where we can't feed the horses, or—"

He points to the North Star, then all the stars in the sky. "Hang loose, Winnie. No matter what happens, we know how it all comes out. We know the ending. We win! You'll see your mom again and all of us and even Jesus. It will be a blast!"

Nickers moves into a gentle canter, jarring loose a verse that fills my head like moonglow. It was Mom's favorite verse and the only one I memorized with her.

And from every corner, mixed with the whisper of the wind and the sound of hooves, the nickers and neighs, I hear *"Amen!"*

Lassoing the Truth

God surprised Winnie with joy and love, bringing in her friends to help and share the joy. When we seek Christ in everything and pay attention, there are no limits to what he might do, or what joy you might share.

Whoa!

Journal to our loving God whatever you're feeling and thinking about him right now.

____

____

____

____

____

____

____

____

____

Dear God, thank you for all the amazing things you've done for me through Jesus Christ. Thank you for giving me joy—in spite of circumstances and because of them.

Giddyup!

Copy Winnie's verse onto a green card. It's a great one to memorize.

Sing to the one who rides across the ancient heavens,
his mighty voice thundering from the sky.
Psalm 68:33

Keep filling your Treasure Box with verses you pick yourself from reading the Bible. Ask your parents, friends, extended family, and church friends to tell you their favorite Bible verses, and add those too. Happy Treasure Hunting!

Wherever your treasure is, there the desires of your heart will also be.

Matthew 6:21

Acknowledgments

Winnie and I love our Tyndale House Publishers team! I always get top-notch editing, design, illustration, development, marketing, and sincere friendships, as well as partnerships. Thanks also to so many faithful and vital employees, from the warehouses to sales and boardrooms. What a blessing it's been to be a Tyndale author for over four decades.

Linda Howard, your enthusiasm and vision and knowledge have guided me from ideas and dream books to real-live books. How can I thank you enough for your friendship?

Debbie King, I'm so grateful for your skillful edits. You have been a partner in many books. Thanks for keeping me from embarrassing myself.

And to my decades-long fan, Jennifer Kozlowski, who made sure I stayed true to the Winnie series—thank you! And thanks to Claire Lloyd for great copyediting, and to Emily Vanderbent, who graciously encourages and arranges for me to connect with readers.

Jackie Nuñez, thanks for sharing your gift of design and your spirit of joy.

Kristen Magnesen, Andrea Martin, and Wendie Connors, what would I do without your tender mercies and support? May I never find out!

For this book, I want to give credit and a shout-out to Talia Messina. You pulled me into writing this journal-devotional in the first place, then showed patience as I thrashed around to get it right. Most of all, thank you for letting me use the Treasure Box in writing each Winnie day! Thanks to your mom for being so wise in creating *your* Treasure Box.

About the Author

Dandi Daley Mackall won her first writing contest as a ten-year-old tomboy. Her fifty words on "Why I Want to Be Batboy for the Kansas City A's" won first place, but the team wouldn't let a girl be a batboy. It was her first taste of rejection.

Since then, Dandi has become an award-winning author of over five hundred books for all ages. She was awarded the Helen Keating Ott Award for Contributions to Children's Literature. Her books have won the Edgar Award for Best Young Adult Mystery, FHL Reader's Choice Award for Long Historical Novel, ALA Best Book for Young Adults, Top Teen Read by NY Public Library, multiple Gold Medallion and Christian Book Awards, and two Mom's Choice Awards.

Dandi was a missionary behind the Iron Curtain in communist-controlled Eastern Europe. Now she is a national speaker, keynoting at conferences, book fairs, and events for all ages, such as at the Jennings Foundation and the International Museum of the Bible in Washington, DC.

She is a frequent guest on podcasts and blogs and makes appearances on radio and TV.

Dandi is the author of the popular Winnie the Horse Gentler series, the Starlight Animal Rescue series, and the Backyard Horses series. She writes from rural Ohio, where she lives with her family, including horses, dogs, cats, a tortoise, a turtle, and visiting squirrels, bunnies, raccoons, deer, and foxes.

Visit Dandi online at:

dandibooks.com

@dandi.mackall

@dandidaleymackall

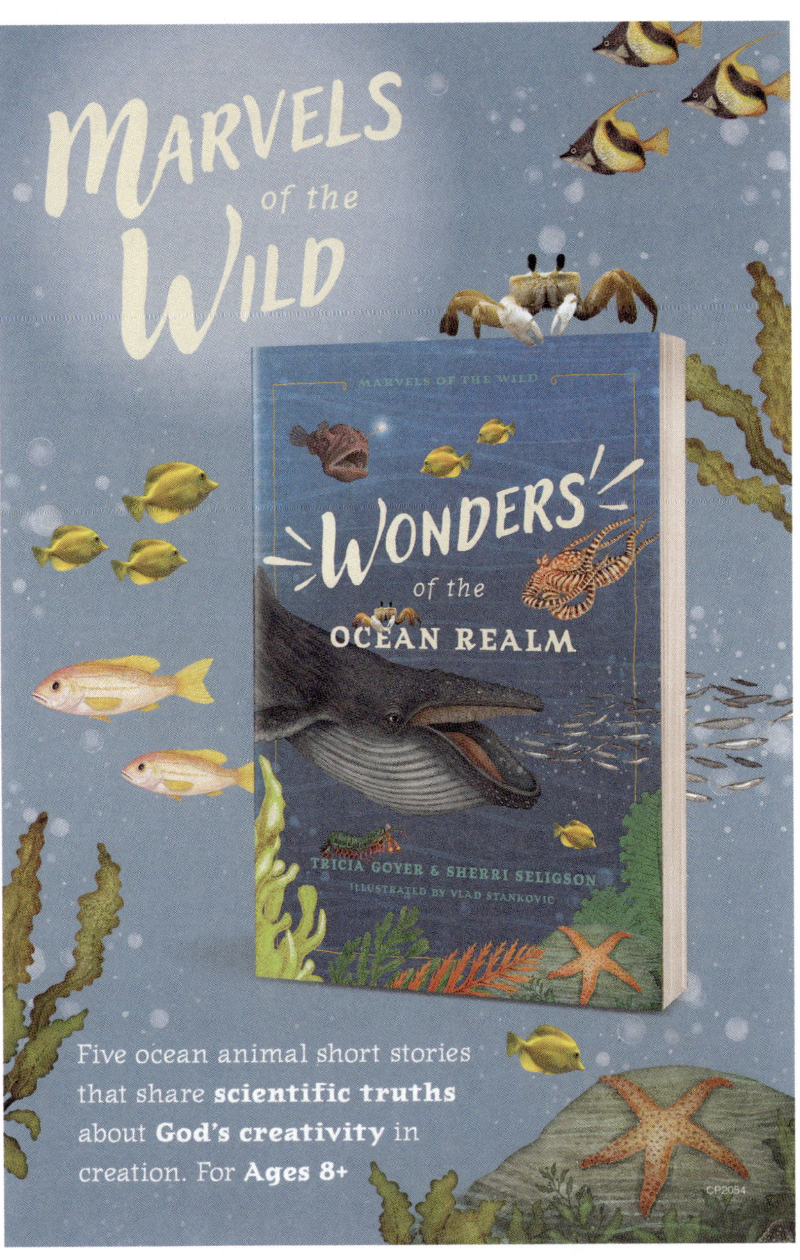

Marvels of the Wild
MARVELS OF THE WILD
WONDERS of the OCEAN REALM
TRICIA GOYER & SHERRI SELIGSON
ILLUSTRATED BY VLAD STANKOVIC
Five ocean animal short stories that share scientific truths about God's creativity in creation. For Ages 8+
CP2054

Hey there! I'm Patrick Wigglesworth. Keep an eye out for all of my Bizarre Bible Adventure books. You won't want to miss a single one!

Book 1
PATRICK WIGGLESWORTH'S Bizarre BIBLE Adventure
Over My Head
Liz and Jack Hagler
Book 2
PATRICK WIGGLESWORTH'S Bizarre BIBLE Adventure
Tricky Times
Liz and Jack Hagler
Book 3
PATRICK WIGGLESWORTH'S Bizarre BIBLE Adventure
Dangerous Dilemmas
Liz and Jack Hagler

CP1890

Don't go nuts waiting to find out what happens to

Get the next book today!

Be on the lookout for more adventures with Merle, Pearl, and all their friends!

CP1478

Join twelve-year-old Winnie Willis and her friends—both human and animal—on their adventures through paddock and pasture as they learn about caring for others, trusting God, and growing up.

Collect all eight Winnie the Horse Gentler books.
Or get the complete collection with the Barn Boxed Set!

CP1423

Saddle Up with Winnie and Friends on the Family Ranch!

tyndale.com/kids

CP1815

STARLIGHT

Animal Rescue

More than just animals need rescuing in this series. Starlight Animal Rescue is where problem horses are trained and loved, where abandoned dogs become heroes, where stray cats become loyal companions—and where people with nowhere to fit in find a place to belong.

#1 Runaway

#2 Mad Dog

#3 Wild Cat

#4 Dark Horse

Read all four to discover how a group of teens cope with life and disappointment.